westermann

W0468191

CAMDEN TOWN

Oberstufe

Arbeitsheft zu den Pflichtmaterialien

Erarbeitet von

Svenja Alpen-Kühne
Anne-Kathrin Böker
Florian Brauel
Ilka Kratz
Alexander Kuhrs Woltin
Jana Oldendörp

Abkürzungen:

AE	American English	*infml.*	informal
BE	British English	*pl.*	plural
e.g.	exempli gratia (Latin) = for example	*sb*	somebody
i.e.	id est (Latin) = that is	*sth*	something

Webcodes
Auf manchen Seiten findest du Webcodes, die dich zu zusätzlichen Materialien im Internet führen. Gib dazu einfach den Code auf www.westermann.de/webcode ins Suchfeld ein.

Filmauszüge
Je nach Abspielgerät und verwendeter Software kann es vorkommen, dass die Zeitangaben zu den Filmauszügen nicht exakt mit den im Kapitel angegebenen übereinstimmen.

Atonement
Die Verweise zu *Atonement* beziehen sich auf diese Ausgabe, die bei Westermann erhältlich ist: Ian McEwan, *Atonement*, ISBN: 978-3-425-73069-1. Kostenlose Annotationen finden sich auf www.westermann.de.

seven methods of killing kylie jenner
Die Verweise zu *seven methods of killing kylie jenner* beziehen sich auf diese Ausgabe, die bei Westermann erhältlich ist: Jasmine Lee-Jones, *seven methods of killing kylie jenner*, ISBN: 978-3-425-73070-7. Kostenlose Annotationen finden sich auf www.westermann.de.

Hamlet
Die Verweise zu *Hamlet* beziehen sich auf diese annotierte Ausgabe: William Shakespeare, *Hamlet*, Westermann 2021, ISBN: 978-3-425-73068-4.

Verweise auf *Skills pages* und *Workshops*
Die Verweise auf *Skills pages* und *Workshops* beziehen sich auf das Schulbuch *Camden Town Oberstufe Qualifikationsphase Niedersachsen*, ISBN: 978-3-425-73642-6.

westermann GRUPPE

Druck A[1] / Jahr 2022
Alle Drucke der Serie A sind im Unterricht parallel verwendbar.

Redaktion: Isabel Klein, Gailingen am Hochrhein
Umschlaggestaltung: Gingco.Net Werbeagentur GmbH & Co. KG, Braunschweig
Layout: Visuelle Lebensfreude, Hannover; thom bahr GRAFIK, Mainz
Druck und Bindung: Westermann Druck GmbH, Georg-Westermann-Allee 66, 38104 Braunschweig

ISBN 978-3-425-**73654**-9

Liebe Schülerin, lieber Schüler,
mit diesem Arbeitsheft kannst du dich ideal auf das Abitur vorbereiten. Du beschäftigst dich mit allen Texten und Filmen, die für das Abitur vorgeschrieben sind, und außerdem mit weiteren abiturrelevanten Themen.

Für das schriftliche Abitur 2024 müssen die folgenden Materialien unter den genannten inhaltlichen Gesichtspunkten behandelt werden:

Roman:
Ian McEwan, *Atonement* (2001)
→ verbindliche Unterrichtsaspekte:
- Britishness
- innocence and guilt
- perception(s) of reality

Film (Berufliche Gymnasien):
John Lee Hancock (Regie), *The Founder* (2016)
→ verbindliche Unterrichtsaspekte:
- American Dream
- ethics in the world of business

Kurzprosa:
Nafissa Thompson-Spires, *Heads of the Colored People: Four Fancy Sketches, Two Chalk Outlines, and No Apology* (2018)
Camille Acker, *Mambo Sauce* (2018)
→ verbindliche Unterrichtsaspekte:
- ethnic identity
- discrimination

Film:
Joel Edgerton (Regie), *Boy Erased* (2018)
→ verbindliche Unterrichtsaspekte:
- coming of age
- sexual diversity
- tolerance and discrimination

Kurzdrama (Allgemein bildende Schulen):
Jasmine Lee-Jones, *seven methods of killing kylie jenner* (2019)
→ verbindliche Unterrichtsaspekte:
- ethnic identity
- the influence of social media on personal life and public opinion

Drama:
Auszüge aus: William Shakespeare, *Hamlet* (ca. 1600)
→ verbindliche Unterrichtsaspekte:
- fate vs. free will
- the role(s) of women
- questions of morality

Aufbau des Arbeitshefts

In **Part 1:** *Atonement*, **Part 2:** *Short stories*, **Part 3:** *The Founder*, **Part 5:** *seven methods of killing kylie jenner* und **Part 6:** *Hamlet* erfolgen zunächst eine inhaltliche Sicherung und allgemeine Bearbeitung der jeweiligen Materialien. Auf speziell ausgewiesenen *Topic*-Seiten werden die verbindlichen Unterrichtsaspekte generell eingeführt, bevor sie im Kontext der jeweiligen Materialien noch einmal vertieft werden. Wo es sich anbietet, werden auch weitere Themen aus dem Lehrplan (Kerncurriculum) aufgegriffen.

In **Part 4:** *Boy Erased* werden zunächst auf *Topic*-Seiten für die Erarbeitung relevante thematische Aspekte behandelt, und dann wird in die Arbeit mit dem Film eingestiegen. Die thematischen Aspekte werden auf zusätzlichen *Topic*-Seiten wieder aufgegriffen und vertieft.

An vielen Stellen findest du Verweise auf *Skills pages* und *Workshops* im Schulbuch *Camden Town Oberstufe Qualifikationsphase* (ISBN: 978-3-425-73642-6). Die *Skills pages* geben dir Hilfestellungen zu wichtigen Aufgabenformaten. In den *Workshops* werden bestimmte Kompetenzen intensiv trainiert. Im Schulbuch werden außerdem weitere Aspekte der Themen dieses Arbeitsheftes behandelt.

Pre-reading

1

You are going to read the novel *Atonement* by Ian McEwan (2001).

a) Read the following quotations. Choose the one that you like best. Explain your choice.

> "The beginning of atonement is the sense of its necessity."
> – *Lord Byron*

> "Forgiveness is not an occasional act, it is a constant attitude."
> – *Martin Luther King Jr.*

> "Always forgive, but never forget, else you will be a prisoner of your own hatred, and doomed to repeat your mistakes forever."
> – *Wil Zeus, Sun Beyond the Clouds*

> "The whole essence of the Christian religion is based on the atonement of Christ, his death and his resurrection."
> – *Gordon B. Hinckley*

> "I guess forgiveness, like happiness, isn't a final destination. You don't one day get there and get to stay."
> – *Deb Caletti*

b) What associations does the title *Atonement* bring to your mind?
What different definitions of the word "atonement" can you find?
Make a mind map and note down your first ideas about the plot of the novel.

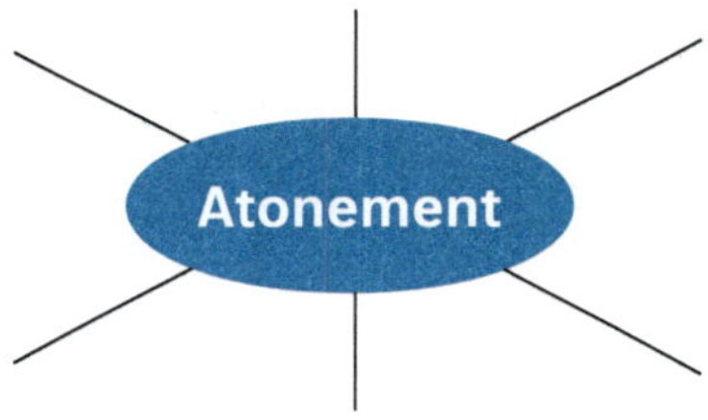

2

a) Use the internet to find out about the author's life.

b) Write a short biography of Ian McEwan for a website on modern English literature.

→ **S8:** How to improve your text

While reading

Info

Keeping a **reading journal** will help you follow and keep track of aspects of a novel such as the plot, the characters and the setting. Your notes will make it easier for you to understand the structure of the novel and the issues it deals with. Initial responses to the text or questions can be noted down, as well as the corresponding lines to help you find the relevant chapters and quotations more quickly. You should take notes in the simple present tense.

3

Now start reading *Atonement*. While reading the book, fill in your reading journal.
Take notes on what you consider to be most important in each section.

Atonement	
Author	
Year of publication	
Genre	
Part One	
Setting (time and place)	
Type of narrator	
Purpose of narrator	
Characters	
Main plot	
Main themes	

Part Two	
Setting (time and place)	
Type of narrator	
Purpose of narrator	
Characters	
Main plot	
Main themes	
Part Three	
Setting (time and place)	
Type of narrator	
Purpose of narrator	

Characters	
Main plot	
Main themes	
London, 1999	
Setting (time and place)	
Type of narrator	
Purpose of narrator	
Characters	
Main plot	
Main themes	

PART ONE: CHAPTER ONE

4

a) Note down facts about the characters mentioned in the first chapter, their relationships and the setting (time and place).
b) Sum up what Briony's play *The Trials of Arabella* is about.
c) Explain why Briony is not enthusiastic about Lola wanting to be Arabella in her play.

5

Describe Briony as she appears in this chapter. Use some of the adjectives from the box. You can add more adjectives if needed.

self-pitying | talented | jealous | naive | selfish | petulant | precocious | childlike | stubborn | bossy | shy | sensitive | talkative | curious | obsessed | stoical | inquisitive | meticulous | devoted | clever | manipulative | kind | ...

6

Examine how the narrator describes Briony and Lola's relationship.

PART ONE: CHAPTERS TWO–THREE

7

Read the statements below. Decide whether the statements are true or false. Tick (✓) the correct box. Provide evidence for each statement. Find a suitable quotation from the novel to support your answer.

Statement		True	False	Quotation
1	The vase is so important to the Tallis family because Jack Tallis's great-great-grandfather made it when visiting Belgium.			
2	Cecilia disrobes and goes swimming for the two missing pieces that have fallen into the fountain after the vase has broken.			
3	When Briony witnesses the scene at the fountain between Robbie and Cecilia, she assumes that Robbie saved her sister from drowning.			
4	Robbie and Cecilia used to be best friends back at university.			

8

Sum up what the reader finds out about Robbie Turner in these chapters.

9

State what Briony means by "The sequence was illogical [...]" (p. 39).

10 Group work → **Workshop:** Analysing characters

a) CHOOSE

Analyse the relationship between Cecilia and Robbie.

OR

Analyse Cecilia's character and her relationship to Briony.

b) Present your results in class.

11

a) To Briony "a story was a form of telepathy" (p. 37). Explain the meaning of this statement.

b) Explain why the scene Briony witnesses at the fountain changes her whole perspective on writing.

c) Analyse the role of the narrator. Why do you think the narrator is going back and retelling the same episode through different eyes?

→ **Workshop:** Analysing narrative perspective

12 Pair work

Think about the significance of the following passage for Briony:
"[...] the simple truth that other people are as real as you. And only in a story could you enter these different minds and show how they had an equal value." (p. 40)
Discuss your ideas with a partner.

PART ONE: CHAPTERS FOUR–SEVEN

13

Match the sentence parts. Write the letters A–F in the boxes.

1	Cecilia attempts to comfort Briony	☐
2	Paul begins flirting with Cecilia	☐
3	Leon and Cecilia start an argument	☐
4	In the nursery,	☐
5	Emily considers her oldest daughter to be an "impossible prospect" (p. 64) as a wife	☐
6	Briony meditates on being a fencing champion instead of becoming a writer	☐

A Paul starts flirting with Lola and tells her and the twins about his chocolate factory.

B when thinking about Cecilia's time at Cambridge.

C while spending time at the temple.

D when Cecilia finds out that Leon has invited Robbie to join them at dinner.

E when she notices her crying in the front hall and destroying her playbill.

F when he enters the house with Leon.

14

Sum up what the reader finds out about Paul Marshall.

15

Examine how Paul Marshall is characterized by the narrator.

16

Describe the Tallis home (place, people, surroundings, atmosphere). Which words are used? What is their effect on the reader?

17 → **Workshop:** Writing an interior monologue

Briony has given up on her play and abandons the rehearsals without any explanation. Write an interior monologue in which she explains her reasons for cancelling the play.

18 → **Workshop:** Analysing characters

Analyse Emily's character as she is portrayed in Chapter Six.

19 Group work

a) CHOOSE

Discuss possible reasons why Jack Tallis doesn't make an appearance in the story.

OR

Discuss whether Emily Tallis could be considered the head of the family.

b) Present your results in class.

PART ONE: CHAPTERS EIGHT–ELEVEN

20

Tick (✓) the correct box to complete each sentence.

1. Robbie writes Cecilia a letter in order to ...
   - ❑ a) confess his love.
   - ❑ b) tell her his sexual desires.
   - ❑ c) apologize for breaking the vase.
   - ❑ d) tell her about his family background.

2. Robbie's father walked out on the family ...
   - ❑ a) because he was called up for military service.
   - ❑ b) because he fell in love with another woman.
   - ❑ c) because he was sent to prison.
   - ❑ d) with no explanation.

3. Robbie asks Briony to pass the letter to Cecilia because ...
   - ❑ a) he doesn't want to give it to Cecilia in front of others.
   - ❑ b) he is ashamed of his feelings for Cecilia.
   - ❑ c) he wants to spend some time alone with Briony.
   - ❑ d) he assumes Cecilia is still upset about the vase and doesn't want to talk to him.

4. When Cecilia asks Briony if she has read the letter, ...
   - ❑ a) Briony admits she has opened the envelope.
   - ❑ b) Briony just ignores Cecilia's inquiry.
   - ❑ c) Briony says the note was passed to her without an envelope.
   - ❑ d) Briony blames Lola for having opened the envelope.

5. Lola starts crying because ...
   - ❑ a) she feels threatened by Paul's attempt to flirt with her.
   - ❑ b) she is homesick.
   - ❑ c) Robbie accuses her of having opened Cecilia's letter.
   - ❑ d) her brothers blame her for being stuck at the Tallises' house.

6. When Briony enters the library and discovers Robbie und Cecilia in an intimate moment, ...
   - ❑ a) she is jealous of her sister because she is in love with Robbie.
   - ❑ b) she believes Cecilia is being attacked and being held by Robbie against her will.
   - ❑ c) she is shocked because her sister is committing a sin.
   - ❑ d) she is embarrassed because she is disrupting an intimate moment.

21

Describe Cecilia and Robbie's relationship.

22

Explain what makes Briony and Lola's relationship change in these chapters.

23
Speculate why Cecilia is not offended by Robbie's letter.

24 Group work
a) CHOOSE
Lola calls Robbie "a maniac" (p. 119) when Briony tells her about the letter. What does this term imply? Discuss.
OR
Robbie decides to go out alone and search for the twins:
"This decision, as he was to acknowledge many times, transformed his life." (p. 144)
Speculate what this last sentence of Chapter Eleven could be foreshadowing.
b) Present your results in class.

PART ONE: CHAPTERS TWELVE–FOURTEEN

25
Organize the information about the Tallis home in a mind map. Try to be as detailed as possible. You can also use information from the previous chapters.

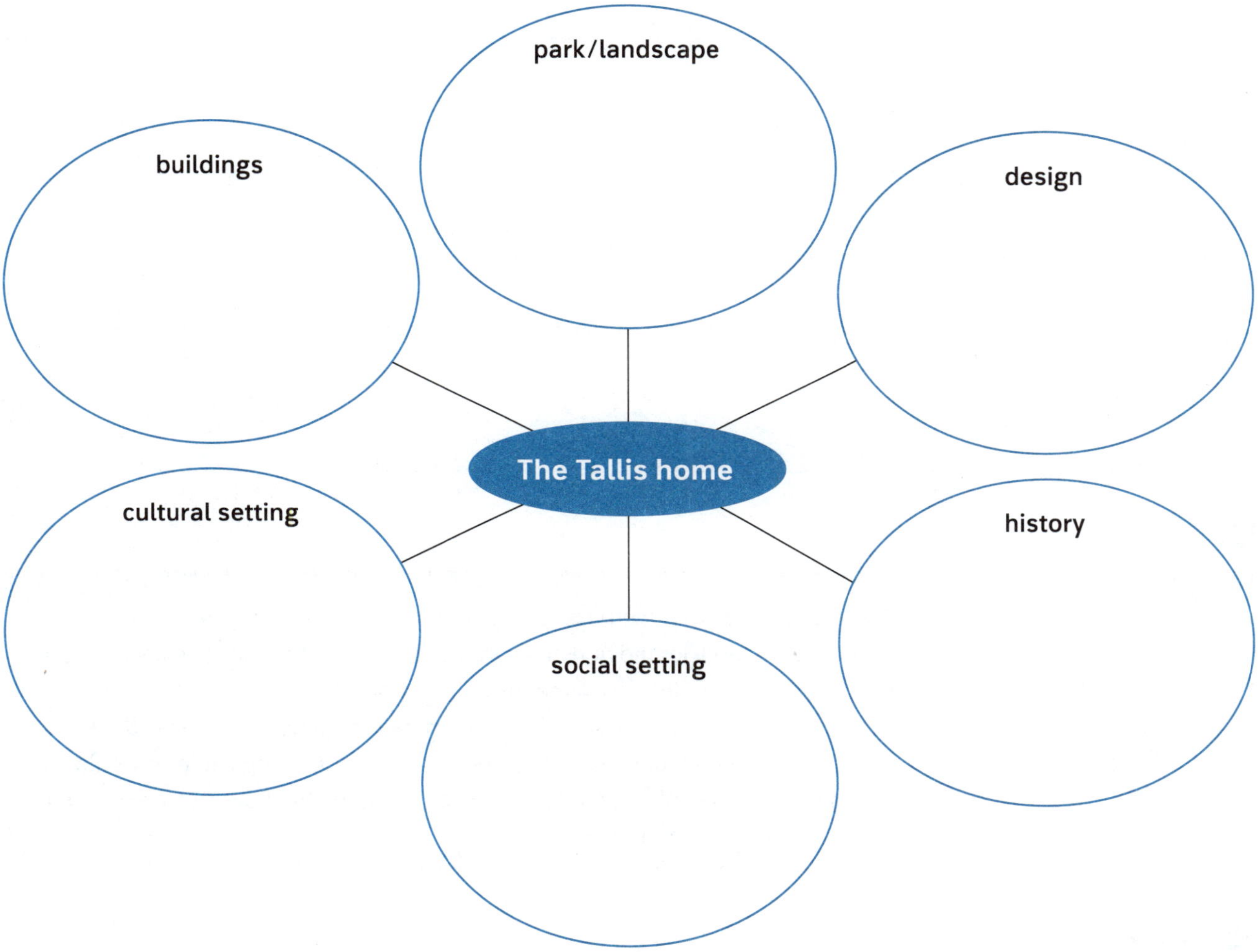

26
Sum up what the reader learns about Jack Tallis.

27
Analyse what Chapter Twelve reveals about the Tallis family and the family members' emotions being repressed.

28

Answer the questions about Chapter Thirteen.

a) Why does Briony make her way towards the island?

b) What happens to Lola by the lake?

c) Why is Briony inferring that Robbie has harmed Lola?

29

a) Read the following information about prolepsis.

b) Examine how this technique is used in Chapters Twelve and Thirteen.

Info

Prolepsis refers to a rhetorical device by which possible objections to an argument are anticipated and answered in advance. The word derives from the Greek "prolambanein", which means "to anticipate".
In literature or film, prolepsis refers to a scene that temporarily takes the story forward in time and represents future events. A modern English term would be "flashforward", revealing crucial aspects of the story that have not yet occurred, but will occur later in the story.

30 → **Workshop:** Analysing narrative perspective

Analyse Briony's perspective of the rape concerning the details included and omitted. Why do you think the author chose her point of view for the narration?

31

Briefly sum up the interrogation and testimony in Chapter Fourteen.

32

Speculate why Briony sticks to her testimony with such unwavering commitment.

33 → **S2:** Checklist: Creative writing

In Chapter Fourteen, a policeman interrogates Briony:
"'You saw him then.'
'I know it was him.'
'Let's forget what you know. You're saying you saw him.'" (p. 181)

a) Imagine Briony not being certain about the suspect and what has happened. How would this change the course of the conversation and the plot?
b) Write an alternative story based on plausible deductions (answering the questions: Who? What? When? Why?).

34 Group work

a) CHOOSE
"How guilt refined the methods of self-torture, threading the beads of detail into an eternal loop, a rosary to be fingered for a lifetime." (p. 173)
Explain this statement and its possible significance for the plot.
OR
"Forgiveness. The word had never meant a thing before, though Briony had heard it exulted at a thousand school and church occasions." (p. 185)
Analyse why this statement could mark a critical turning point in Briony's biography. How and why does "forgiveness" acquire a new meaning for her?
b) Present your results in class.

35

In class, discuss the importance of Briony being the only witness to the crime.

36 → **Workshop:** Analysing narrative perspective

Explain the role of the narrator in Part One. Speculate why the author chose this narrative style.

PART TWO

37

The Second World War is used as a setting in the second part of the novel.
a) Use the internet to find out about "Dunkirk 1940".
b) Use the information to fill in the fact file.

Dunkirk 1940	
Who?	
When?	
Where?	
Why?	
How?	

38

Read the statements below. Decide whether the statements are true or false. Tick (✓) the correct box. Provide evidence for each statement.

Statement		True	False	Evidence
1	Robbie Turner and Corporals Mace and Nettle take refuge in the barn of an old French woman.			
2	They have to stay in Dunkirk because they weren't able to catch a Naval ship back to England.			
3	Turner is haunted by nightmares because of his time in prison and his war experiences.			
4	While Robbie Turner was imprisoned, Cecilia remained supportive of his innocence.			
5	When Robbie and Cecilia meet again at a café in London, their relationship is still strong.			
6	Robbie forgives the Tallis family for putting him to prison and encourages Cecilia to reach out to her family.			
7	After an aerial assault, Turner denies his major's orders to sneak-attack the German machine gun location.			
8	Turner recalls a summer day in 1932 when Briony faked a drowning to test Robbie to see if he would save her because she is in love with him.			
9	Turner successfully rescues a boy and his mother as the bomber nears.			
10	Turner's wound leads to his strong delusion.			

39
Describe the change in setting (time and place) that takes place in Part Two of the novel.

40
"There were horrors enough, but it was the unexpected detail that threw him and afterwards would not let him go." (p. 191)
Contrast the narrative style at the beginning of Part Two to the one in Part One.

41
Examine how the narrator shows the horror of war and its consequences using implicit words and pictures. Find suitable examples from the text.

42 Group work

a) CHOOSE

"I keep thinking of her. To go into nursing, to cut herself off from her background, is a bigger step for her than it was for me." (p. 212)
Analyse the importance of family for both Robbie and Cecilia taking into account background knowledge from Part One.

OR

"He wanted a father, and for the same reason, he wanted to be a father. It was common enough, to see so much death and want a child." (p. 241)
Examine why seeing the horrors of war makes Robbie long for an intact world.

b) Present your results in class.

43 Pair work
Discuss why the narrator draws the reader's attention to the acts of kindness by Turner, Mace and Nettle. What might this reveal about their characters?

44 → **S2:** Checklist: Creative writing
Reread Cecilia's letter in which she tells Robbie that everyone has turned on him (p. 209). Write Robbie's reply to Cecilia's letter.

45
The narrator relates Robbie and Cecilia to some other famous romantic couples who have overcome all odds for their love (p. 204).

a) List the couples and find background information on them.
b) Discuss why the narrator brings up those couples. What does this tell the reader about Robbie and Cecilia's relationship?

46
Describe and analyse what the reader learns about Briony in Part Two of the novel.

47 Group work
Imagine you were turning Cecilia and Robbie's reunion at the café (pp. 204–207) into a short screenplay.

a) Answer the following questions to prepare the screenplay.
- What would the stage look like?
- How would the actors be dressed?
- What would the actors say? Refer to Robbie and Cecilia's conversation in the text.

b) Act out the scene.

PART THREE

48

Answer the following questions about Part Three.

a) What made Briony become a nurse?

b) Why has Briony detached herself from her family?

c) Why does Briony keep a journal?

d) How does Briony react when she gets to know that Paul and Lola are getting married?

e) How does Briony cope with taking care of wounded soldiers returning from the war?

f) Why does Briony visit the church where Paul and Lola are getting married?

g) What happens when Briony visits Cecilia's apartment?

49
Describe the shift in narrative style in Part Three compared to the previous parts.

50
Examine the fact that Betty drops Uncle Clem's vase on the steps (p. 279). What could this incident represent?

51 → **Workshop:** Analysing atmosphere
"The unease was not confined to the hospital. It seemed to rise with the turbulent brown river swollen by the April rains, and in the evenings lay across the blacked-out city like a mental dusk which the whole country could sense, a quiet and malign thickening, inseparable from the cool late spring, well concealed within its spreading beneficence. Something was coming to an end." (p. 269)
State what imagery is used to create a sense of unease in the reader about what is going to happen at the hospital.

52
Reread the letter on pp. 311–315.
Sum up what CC criticizes about Briony's story.

Info
The initials "CC" stand for Cyril Connolly (1903–1974), an influential English literary critic and writer. He founded and edited the important literary magazine *Horizon*.

53
Write Briony's reply to CC's letter.
→ **S2:** Checklist: Creative writing
→ **S3:** Checklist: Formal letter

54
Reread the end of Part Three and speculate how the story could go on.
"She knew what was required of her. Not simply a letter, but a new draft, an atonement, and she was ready to begin.

BT
London 1999" (p. 349)

55

Did World War II hinder Briony from atoning or rather enable her to do so? Discuss in class.

LONDON, 1999

56

Sum up what happens in the final section of the novel.

57

Reread the lines from *The Trials of Arabella* on pp. 367–368. Analyse why Briony's teenage play appears again at the end of the novel.

58

Briony has just been diagnosed with vascular dementia (pp. 353–355).

a) Use the internet to gather information on vascular dementia.

b) Assess the significance of the fact that Briony is suffering from vascular dementia. Does this affect her credibility as a writer/narrator/person trying to atone?

c) **Group work**
Discuss whether Briony's disease could be seen as a kind of salvation or a punishment for her crime.

59 **Group work**

Reread the scene when Briony returns to her former home (pp. 363–365). Compare the description of the place in this chapter with the Tallis home in Part One.

60 **Group work**

"I've been thinking about my last novel, the one that should have been my first. The earliest version, January 1940, the latest, March 1999, and in between, half a dozen different drafts." (p. 369)
"It is only in this last version that my lovers end well, standing side by side on a South London pavement as I walk away." (p. 370)
Discuss what Briony's statement at the end of the novel implies for the story as a whole and the reliability of the narrator. You can also use information from the previous pages (especially pp. 356–360) and the box below.

Info

An **unreliable narrator** is usually a first-person narrator and character within the story whose narration and perception are not completely credible due to the character's affected mental condition or maturity. As a result, this narrator has a distorted view of events, gives illogical or contradicting information and speaks with a bias or even lies.
Accordingly, a **reliable narrator** is considered a credible storyteller being fully aware of the circumstances around him/her. His/Her perception of the world is trustworthy and coherent.
Reliable and unreliable narration has been widely debated within literary scholarship since some literary critics argue that there is no such thing as a reliable first-person narrator at all. According to them, every literary character is affected by his or her past experiences and perception in the telling of a story. However, generally most first-person narrators attempt to give the most accurate and therefore reliable version of the events told in the story. One reason for creating an unreliable narrator is to make the reader reconsider their point of view and create dramatic suspense by making the truth unclear.

61

"The problem these fifty-nine years has been this: how can a novelist achieve atonement when, with her absolute power of deciding outcomes, she is also God? There is no one, no entity or higher form that she can appeal to, or be reconciled with, or that can forgive her. There is nothing outside her." (p. 371)
Explain why Briony compares her novelist self to God.

Post-reading

62 Group work

Comment on the ending of the novel. Who does Briony seek atonement from?

63 Group work

Discuss the thematic focus of the novel. Is it a novel about ...?

identity | coming of age | perception | social class | redemption | innocence | guilt | war

Find arguments for and against the different options.

64 → **Workshop:** Analysing characters → **S8:** How to improve your text

Choose one of the following characters and write a characterization.

- Cecilia Tallis
- Emily Tallis
- Robbie Turner
- Paul Marshall

65 Group work

Discuss the importance of water in the novel. Find passages that relate to water and are crucial to the course of the story.

66 Group work

Discuss how the theme of war and its consequences is presented in the novel.

67 → **Workshop:** Analysing characters

Analyse the development of Briony throughout the novel.

68 Group work

Reread the final two paragraphs of the novel (pp. 371–372). Discuss whether Briony successfully atones for the events in 1935 by writing her novel.

69

a) Read the review on *Atonement* from *The Guardian*. Discuss whether (or not) you agree with the review.

b) Write your own review of the novel. → **S8:** How to improve your text

GEOFF DYER **Sat 22 Sep 2001**

Who's afraid of influence?

In his latest book Atonement Ian McEwan brings the British novel into the 21st century, says Geoff Dyer

The twists and turns of Ian McEwan's fiction are built on a knack for sustained illusion. When he writes "a glass of beer" we do not just see it; we are willing to drink from it vicariously. The ballooning accident (imaginatively derived from footage of an actual incident) that opens Enduring Love is a spectacular example, but the ability to make the invented seem real animates every page of his work.

The novels' psychological acuity[1] derives, always, from their fidelity to a precisely delineated[2] reality. Needless to say, the more disturbing or skewed that reality (in the early stories and novels, most obviously), the more finely McEwan attunes his readers to it. Moral ambiguity and doubt are thereby enhanced – rather than resolved – by clarity of presentation. This is why the themes of the novels (with the exception of the enjoyably

Annotations

[1] **acuity** = *Schärfe*

[2] **delineated** = *skizziert*

forgettable Amsterdam) linger and resonate beyond the impeccable[3] neatness of their arrangement. McEwan is, in other words, a thoroughly traditional original.

Atonement does not feel, at first, like a book by McEwan. The opening is almost perversely ungripping. Instead of the expected sharpness of focus, the first 70 or so pages are a lengthy summary of shifting impressions. One longs for a cinematic clarity and concentration of dialogue and action, but such interludes dissolve before our – and the participants' – eyes. [...]

Various characters come and go but the novel, at this point, seems populated mainly by its literary influences. Chief among these is Virginia Woolf[4]. The technique is not stream of consciousness so much as "a slow drift of association", "the hovering stillness of nothing much seeming to happen". The book later contains a critique of its own early pages – or at least of the draft from which they derive – in the guise of a letter from Cyril Connolly, editor of Horizon, who advises that "such writing can become precious when there is no sense of forward movement". The requisite propulsion is provided by the unexpected intrusion, as it were, of two other novelists from the interwar years.

Cecilia, the eldest daughter of the family in whose house we are imaginatively lodged, was at Cambridge with Robbie, the son of the Tallises' cleaning lady, whose education was funded by Cecilia's father. They become aware, on this sultry day, of some kind of current – animosity? irreconcilable attraction? – passing between them. Robbie tries to articulate this in a letter, at the bottom of which he scribbles the naked truth: "In my dreams I kiss your cunt." He discards that draft and intends to send another, blander one but, in keeping with Freud's analysis of such slips, accidentally sends the shocking letter to Cecilia via her adolescent sister, Briony, who opens and reads it. [...]

Another crisis soon follows, this one imported from EM Forster's India. Cecilia's young cousin, Lola, is sexually assaulted in the grounds of the house. Lola does not know by whom, but Briony – an aspiring writer – compounds her earlier transgression[5] by convincing her and everyone else (except Cecilia) that Robbie is the culprit. Unlike the incident in the Marabar caves, this one does not end in a retraction and Robbie, the proletarian interloper, is convicted.

In the second section of the novel, the pastel haze of the first part gives way to an acrid[6], graphic account of Robbie's later experiences in the British rout at Dunkirk. McEwan is here playing more obviously to his strengths. The highly decorated novelist deploys his research in an effective if familiar pattern of narrative manoeuvres. Refracted through Robbie's exhausted, wounded view of history in the making, the retreat unfolds in a series of vividly realised details and encounters. In the atrocious context of battle, Briony's apparently motiveless crime is rendered almost insignificant. "But what was guilt these days? It was cheap. Everyone was guilty, and no one was."

In similar fashion, the partial democratisation of Britain that results from the social upheaval of war is prefigured by Cecilia's turning her back on her family and allying herself with Robbie, the working-class graduate (whose smouldering sense of grievance and displacement would be vehemently embodied on the postwar stage by Jimmy Porter).

Part three shifts back to London, where Briony is training as a nurse, struggling to cope with the influx of casualties from Dunkirk. McEwan's command of visceral shock is here anchored in a historical setting thoroughly authenticated by his archival imagination. The elliptical style of the opening part has no place in these pages, as the graphic horrors of injury, mutilation and death pile up before Briony's eyes. She loosens the bandage around a patient's head and his brain threatens to slop out into her hands. Does this devotion to the victims of war wash her hands of her earlier guilt? Does her atonement depend on Robbie's survival? Or can it be achieved through the eventual realisation of her literary ambitions – through a novel such as the one we are reading? Who can grant atonement to the novelist, whose God-like capacity to create and rework the world means that there is no higher authority to whom appeal can be made?

It is a tribute to the scope, ambition and complexity of Atonement that it is difficult to give an adequate sense of what is going on in the novel without preempting – and thereby diminishing – the reader's experience of it. Suffice to say, any initial hesitancy about style – any fear that, for once, McEwan may not be not in control of his material – all play their part in his larger purpose. [...]

Annotations

[3] **impeccable** = *tadellos*

[4] **Virginia Woolf** (1882–1941) was a British writer. She is considered one of the most important authors of modernist literature. She experimented with different forms of writing and was a pioneer in using stream of consciousness as a narrative device.

[5] **transgression** = *Verstoß, Überschreitung*

[6] **acrid** = *beißend, scharf*

ATONEMENT – THE FILM: PRE-VIEWING

70

Atonement was turned into a romantic war drama film, released in 2007. It was directed by Joe Wright, starring James McAvoy, Keira Knightley, Romola Garai, Saoirse Ronan, Vanessa Redgrave and Benedict Cumberbatch.
Describe the film poster and identify the characters shown.

____

____

____

____

____

WHILE VIEWING

71

Watch the film. Answer the following questions.

a) What is Briony like in the film?

____

____

____

b) How is Cecilia shown in the film?

____

____

____

c) What happens to the frame story?

____

____

____

POST-VIEWING

72 Group work

a) Compare the ending of the novel to the final scenes of the film.
b) Discuss to what extent the film and the novel differ in terms of concepts of atonement.

73 Pair work

Novel or film? Discuss which of the two versions of *Atonement* you prefer. Justify your opinion.

Britishness

1 → **S15:** How to describe pictures
Describe the pictures below. Which aspects of British tradition and culture are depicted?

2
Read the findings from the research study "Citizenship and Belonging: What is Britishness?" by the Commission for Racial Equality (2005).

What is Britishness?
Most of the research participants shared a common representation of Britishness, ranging over eight dimensions:

- **Geography:** Britishness was associated with the British Isles, and with typical topographic features, such as the Scottish Highlands, lochs, Welsh valleys, and rolling hills.
- **National symbols:** Britishness was symbolised by the Union Jack and the royal family.
- **People:** Three different ways of thinking about the British people emerged: for some participants, the British included all British citizens (that is, those who hold UK passports), regardless of region or ethnicity; for others, the British were exclusively associated with white English people; and for others still, the British included people of very diverse ethnic origins.
- **Values and attitudes:** These included upholding human rights and freedoms, respect for the rule of law, fairness, tolerance and respect for others, reserve and pride (generally valued by white English participants and criticised by white Scottish and white Welsh participants, as well as those from ethnic minority backgrounds), a strong work ethic, community spirit, mutual help, stoicism and compassion, and drunkenness, hooliganism and yobbishness.
- **Cultural habits and behaviour:** These included queuing; watching and supporting football, cricket and rugby; and consuming food and drink such as 'fish and chips', 'English breakfast', 'Yorkshire pudding', 'cream teas', 'cucumber sandwiches', 'roast beef', 'Sunday lunch', 'curries' and 'beer'.
- **Citizenship:** For Scottish and Welsh participants, and for most participants from ethnic minority backgrounds, Britishness was very much associated with holding a UK passport. This was not salient among white English participants.
- **Language:** English was seen as a common language that unites the British people. The array of British accents (in terms of regional and class differences) was also seen as typically British.

- **Achievements:** Britishness was associated with political and historical achievements (the establishment of parliamentary democracy, empire and colonialism); technological and scientific achievements (the industrial revolution, medical discoveries); sporting achievements (the invention of many sports); and 'pop' cultural achievements.

Identification with Britishness

While the content of 'Britishness' was shared across most groups, there were important differences in the ways in which participants personally related to, and identified with, Britishness.

As UK passport holders, all the participants *knew* they were British citizens, but not everyone attached any *value significance* to being British. In Scotland and Wales, white and ethnic minority participants identified more strongly with each of those countries than with Britain. In England, white English participants perceived themselves as English first and as British second, while ethnic minority participants perceived themselves as British; none identified as English, which they saw as meaning exclusively white people. Thus, the participants who identified most strongly with Britishness were those from ethnic minority backgrounds resident in England. [...]

3 → **S8:** How to improve your text

Write your own definition of the term "Britishness" using additional information from the internet.

MEDIATION

4 → **Workshop:** Mediation → **S19:** How to improve your mediation skills → **S7:** Checklist: Writing a blog post

Imagine you are an exchange student at a school in Britain. Your class is doing a project on Britishness and patriotism. You are asked to contribute a German perspective on the matter and found an article from *Der Spiegel*. Read the article below and write a blog post for the school website.

Wie ein Schülerlied Großbritannien entzweit

„Untersteht euch, meinem Kind das Gehirn zu waschen!“

Der britische Bildungsminister wünscht sich, dass in allen Schulen am Freitag ein patriotisches Lied gesungen wird. In Schottland und anderen Landesteilen fühlen sich viele an Nordkorea oder die DDR erinnert.

Von Jörg Schindler, London *24.06.2021, 20.12 Uhr*

„Wenn die Musik der Liebe Nahrung ist, spielt weiter“, schrieb William Shakespeare – aber der hatte auch gut reden. Als der Barde vor mehr als 400 Jahren zur Feder griff, gab es noch kein Vereinigtes Königreich. Und erst recht keinen Brexit. Im heutigen Großbritannien würde womöglich gar Shakespeare lieber betroffen schweigen, bevor er einen Shitstorm riskiert.

Im heutigen Großbritannien ist öffentliches Gezänk über ein Lied entbrannt, das Außenstehenden schwer vermittelbar ist. Also das Gezänk. Wobei: das Lied eigentlich auch.

Geschrieben haben es angeblich Schüler der St. John's Primary School im englischen Bradford. Es handelt von einer großen Inselnation, die „viele Stürme und viele Kriege“ überlebt, ihre Grenzen in der Welt „erweitert“ hat und dabei „immer geeint, niemals entzweit“ auftrat. Es endet mit der inbrünstig und gleich viermal hintereinander vorgetragenen Zeile: „Strong Britain, Great Nation“ – starkes Britannien, große Nation. [...]

Das Problem mit dem Lied ist nun jedoch nicht, dass es eine gewisse patriotische Schlagseite der Heranwachsenden von Bradford offenbart. Das Problem ist, dass es am morgigen Freitag möglichst in allen Schulen des Vereinigten Königreichs

gesungen werden soll. Idealerweise von in Rot, Weiß und Blau gewandeten Kindern – den Farben des Union Jack.
So wünscht es sich die kleine Initiative „One Britain One Nation", die nicht zufällig ebenfalls aus Bradford stammt und den letzten Freitag im Juni zum „One Britain One Nation Day" erklärt hat. So wünscht es sich auch der britische Bildungsminister Gavin Williamson, der im britischen Parlament wissen ließ, er halte es für „unglaublich wichtig", dass die Schulen des Landes dem Aufruf folgen. [...]
Seit Williamson dem Kinderlied ausgerechnet am fünften Jahrestag des Brexit-Referendums quasi den Regierungsstempel aufgedrückt hat, kann von einem immer einigen, niemals entzweiten Königreich keine Rede mehr sein. In den sozialen Netzwerken machten sogleich Fotomontagen die Runde, die Williamsons Chef als Kim Jong-Johnson zeigten. [...]
Vor allem aber kommen der Song und seine Begleitumstände in jenen drei Landesteilen des Vereinigten Königreichs, bei denen es sich nicht um England handelt, weniger gut an. In Schottland, Wales und Nordirland betrachtet man den chauvinistischen Überschwang, mit dem Johnson und seine Brexitclique das Land seit geraumer Zeit überziehen, mit wachsendem Befremden. [...]
Dass die Regierenden in London neuerdings auf jedem Regierungsgebäude den Union Jack sehen wollen, dass sie für schlappe 200 Millionen Pfund das National-Flaggschiff „Britannia" nachbauen lassen, dass zuletzt jede Kritik am britischen Kolonialreich und seinem profitablen Sklavenhandel regierungsamtlich niederkartätscht wurde, ist selbst manchem Brexitfreund nicht mehr ganz geheuer.
In bester Erinnerung ist vielen auch noch die boshafte Auseinandersetzung von Ministern Ihrer Majestät mit der BBC, die im vergangenen Jahr den traditionellen Schlussakkord des Klassikfestivals „Proms" – „Rule Britannia" – in seiner bisherigen Form aus dem Programm streichen wollte. Über Wochen mussten sich BBC-Journalisten dafür als vaterlandslose Gesellen beschimpfen lassen.
Nun also setzt sich der Streit auf Grundschulniveau fort. Mit einer gewissen Fassungslosigkeit wiesen Vertreter der britischen Teilnationen darauf hin, dass der patriotische Ohrwurm aus Bradford eher das Zeug zum Spalten als zum Vereinen habe. So sei Nordirland mit dem Slogan „Strong Britain" schlicht vergessen worden. Nicht von ungefähr laute der offizielle Name des Landes: Vereinigtes Königreich von Großbritannien UND Nordirland. [...]
Die Schotten wiederum finden es typisch Englisch, dass der Song ausgerechnet am Freitag landesweit geträllert werden soll – just an jenem Tag, an dem schottische Schüler bereits in den Ferien sind oder geschickt werden sollen. Und in Wales wiesen Lehrer und Eltern darauf hin, dass Erziehung eine originäre Zuständigkeit der Regionen sei, man aber von niemandem vorab informiert worden sei.
Die Stimmung dort brachte eine Mutter ganz gut auf den Punkt, die über soziale Medien wissen ließ: „Untersteht euch, meinem Kind das Gehirn zu waschen! Vier Nationen – Cymru am byth". Das ist Walisisch für „Lang lebe Wales".
Im englischen Bradford saß derweil ein einigermaßen indignierter Kash Singh, jener Mann, der die Initiative „One Britain One Nation" vor acht Jahren ersonnen hat. Die Reaktionen auf das gut gemeinte Lied seien „diabolisch", seufzte der Ex-Polizist. Man lebe doch gemeinsam in einem „brillanten Land", und es sei notwendig, den dort herrschenden „Geist der Einheit und des Zusammenhalts" gelegentlich zu feiern.
Die Frage muss allerdings erlaubt sein: Von welchem Geist redet der Mann?

BRITISHNESS IN *ATONEMENT*

5

Reread Chapter Twelve in Part One of the novel. Sum up and identify characteristics about the Tallis household that can be considered typically British.

6

Social context and social class are an important setting in the novel. Examine to what extent social context and class matters are related to Britishness in the novel.

7
Part Two deals intensively with central events of the Second World War from a British perspective. When Robbie and the other soldiers meet a major from the Buffs (a regiment of the British Army), he is depicted as follows:

"The major had a little toothbrush moustache overhanging small, tight lips that clipped his words briskly. 'We've got Jerry trapped in the woods over there. He must be an advance party. But he's well dug in with a couple of machine guns. We're going to get in there and flush him out.'
Turner felt the horror chill and weaken his legs. He showed the major his empty palms.
'What with, sir?'
'With cunning and a bit of teamwork.'
How was the fool to be resisted? Turner was too tired to think, though he knew he wasn't going." (p. 220)

Examine how the major resembles the stereotype of a British gentleman. Speculate why the author created this character as part of the novel.

8 Pair work
Is it important that the story is (for the most part) set in England? Discuss your ideas with a partner and justify your answer.

Innocence and guilt

1
Look at the cartoon and describe it. What does it tell you about innocence in relation to guilt?

2 Pair work
Explain the message of the cartoon and its reference to the novel.

→ **Workshop:** Analysing a cartoon
→ **S17:** How to work with cartoons

3
Look up definitions of the words "innocence" and "guilt". How do they differ in meaning and connotation?

"It's innocent or guilty. There are no do-overs."

INNOCENCE AND GUILT IN *ATONEMENT*

4
Speculate who else could be at fault for the crime committed in the summer of 1935.
Is Briony the only one who should feel guilty? Is Lola guilty for not saying anything? What role do their parents play?

5
Explain why Briony made a false statement (pp. 173–183). Can you understand why she acted as she did?

6 Pair work
Briony is only thirteen when she is interviewed by the police. Discuss the role of adults in Part One of the novel. Why do adults fully rely on the observation of a child?

7 Pair work

Reread the end of Part Two (pp. 261–265). Examine the significance of innocence and guilt for Robbie. You can also use information from other chapters.

8

In class, discuss whether the outbreak of the Second World War in Part Two of the novel can be seen as a loss of innocence in broader scope.

Perception(s) of reality

1 → **S15:** How to describe pictures

Describe the picture.

2

Explain its message and what it tells us about the perception(s) of reality.

3

Comment on the following quote.

> "Perception is more important than reality. If someone perceives something to be true, it is more important than if it is in fact true."
> – *Ivanka Trump, The Trump Card*

What dangers might be in this opinion?

PERCEPTION(S) OF REALITY IN *ATONEMENT*

4 Group work

An essential theme of *Atonement* is the way an individual's perspective shapes the perception of reality.

a) Go back to Part One, Chapters Two and Three. Sum up how the fountain scene is perceived differently by Cecilia and Briony.

b) Examine the significance of the mirror in Chapter Nine.

c) Analyse how Briony perceives crucial events (for example, the scene at the fountain, the scene in the library, the assault by the lake and Robbie's arrest in front of the house) in Part One.

5 Pair work

Analyse how your interpretations of the characters alter once you know that Briony is the author of the novel.

→ **Workshop:** Analysing characters → **Workshop:** Analysing narrative perspective

6

Atonement is said to be a narrative within a narrative. Comment on this statement.

7

"I know there's always a certain kind of reader who will be compelled to ask, But what *really* happened?" (p. 371)

In class, discuss how you would answer the question of what really happened.

Heads of the Colored People: Four Fancy Sketches, Two Chalk Outlines, and No Apology – A short story (2018)

PRE-READING

1

Below is the title of the short story you are going to read. Read it step by step. Make predictions about what each part might reveal about the plot of the story.

"Heads of the Colored People":

___

"Four Fancy Sketches":

___

"Two Chalk Outlines":

___

"and No Apology":

___

2

Read the information about the main characters. Try to predict what their roles in the plot of the story might be.

Riley: A young black man with bleached-blond hair; he loves dressing himself up as characters from his favourite books, movies, manga and anime series.

___

___

Brother Man: A black man whose real name is Richard Simmons; he hands out pamphlets in the street and is ignored by Riley, which he can't handle.

___

Kevan Peterson: Father of five-year-old Penny; he is on his way to a meeting to pitch a business idea concerning black art.

___

Paris Larkin: Riley's girlfriend; she is a sketch artist who calls her sketchbooks "a collection of heads" because she never draws bodies.

___

___

Heads of the Colored People: Four Fancy Sketches, Two Chalk Outlines, and No Apology

by Nafissa Thompson-Spires

1.

Riley wore blue contact lenses and bleached his hair — which he worked with gel and a blow-dryer and a flatiron[1] some mornings into Sonic the Hedgehog[2] spikes so stiff you could prick[3] your finger on them, and sometimes into a wispy[4] side-swooped bob with long bangs — and he was black. But this wasn't any kind of self-hatred thing. He'd read *The Bluest Eye*[5] and *Invisible Man*[6] in school and even picked up *Disgruntled*[7] at a book fair, and yes, they were good and there was some resonance in those books for him, but this story isn't about race or "the shame of being alive" or any of those things. He was not self-hating; he was even listening to Drake — though you could make it Fetty Wap[8] if his appreciation for trap music changes something for you, because all that's relevant here is that he wasn't against the music of "his people" or anything like that — as he walked down Figueroa[9] with his earbuds pushed in just far enough so as not to feel itchy.

Riley was wearing the wispy swooped version of his bangs[10] and listening to Drake or Fetty, and he was black with blue contacts and bleached-blond hair. And, yes, there are black people who have both of those things naturally, without the use of artificial accouterments[11], so we can move past the whole phenotypically this or biologically that discussion to the meat of things[12]. And if there is something meta in this narrator's consciousness and self-consciousness or this overindulgent[13] aside, it isn't meta for the sake of being meta; this narrator's consciousness is just letting you know about said consciousness up front, like a raised black fist, to get the close reading out the way and make space for Riley, who was the kind of black man for whom blue eyes and blond hair were not natural. He was the kind of black that warranted — or invited without solicitation — comparisons to drinks from Starbucks or lyrics from "Lady Marmalade"[14] or chocolate bars, with nuts.

You would think with his blue contacts and unnaturally blond hair set against dark chocolate mocha-choca-latte-yaya skin — and yes, there is some judgment in the use of "you" — that Riley would date white or Asian women exclusively, or perhaps that he liked men. But you'd be wrong on all counts[15], as Riley was straight, and he dated widely among black women, and he was neither in denial, nor on the down-low, nor, like John Mayer[16], equal opportunity and United Colors of Benetton in life but as separate as the fingers of the hand in sex, nor like Frederick Douglass[17] or many others working on black rights in public and going home to a white wife (and there is no judgment against Douglass here, just facts for the sake of descriptive clarity). Riley liked black women, both their blackness and womanness and the overlap between those constructs; nor was Riley queerphobic[18] or the type of man to utter "no homo" in uncomfortable situations, because Riley was comfortable enough, if "enough" expresses a sort of educated awareness. There is so much awareness in these two paragraphs that I have hardly made space for Riley, who in addition to black women liked cosplay[19] — dressing up as characters from his favorite books and movies — and *Dr. Who*[20] and *Rurouni Kenshin*[21] and the Comic-Love convention, and especially *Death Note*, his favorite manga and anime series. And though that day he was dressed as Tamaki Suoh[22] (per his girlfriend's request), in a skinny periwinkle[23] suit with a skinny black tie, his appearance gave him the flexibility to on other occasions dress as Kise Ryouta[24] or Naruto[25], or, if he was feeling especially bold, Super Saiyan[26].

So it was bothersome, then, to Riley/Tamaki as he walked

Annotations

1 **flatiron** = a hot tool to straighten hair
2 **Sonic the Hedgehog** = the main character of a video game series
3 to **prick** = to stick into your skin and cause you pain
4 **wispy** = fine, thin
5 ***The Bluest Eye*** = title of a novel written by Toni Morrison
6 ***Invisible Man*** = title of a novel written by Ralph Ellison
7 ***Disgruntled*** = title of a novel written by Asali Solomon
8 **Fetty Wap** = an American rapper
9 **Figueroa** = a major north-south street in Los Angeles County, California
10 **bangs** = a hairstyle with the hair being cut so that it hangs over your forehead
11 **accouterments** = accessories
12 **the meat of things** = (figurative) the most important part of a topic
13 **overindulgent** = excessive, having more of something than is good for you
14 **"Lady Marmalade"** = a song recorded in 1974 by the American R&B group Labelle
15 **on all counts** = in every way
16 **John Mayer** = an American singer, songwriter and guitarist
17 **Frederick Douglass** was an African-American social reformer, statesman and writer in the 19th century. He became famous for his anti-slavery writings.
18 **queerphobic** = fearing or hating queer people
19 **cosplay** = short for: costume play
20 ***Doctor Who*** = a famous British science-fiction TV series
21 ***Rurouni Kenshin*** = a Japanese manga series
22 **Tamaki Suoh** = a character from the manga and anime series *Ouran High School Host Club*
23 **periwinkle** = lavender blue
24 **Kise Ryouta** = a character from a Japanese sports manga series
25 **Naruto** = a character (a young ninja) from a Japanese manga series
26 **Super Saiyan** = a form of transformation in the Japanese manga and anime series *Dragon Ball*

toward the Los Angeles Convention Center, when Brother Man at the corner of Figueroa and Fifteenth — not to be confused with the Original Bruh Man, whose actual origins or current whereabouts are unknown, but Bruh Man's gradated type, this particular yet stock Bruh Man, Brother Man — accosted[27] Riley after he brushed away the pamphlet Brother Man was trying to hand him and put his hand on Riley's shoulder and ventured to violate Riley's personal space even further by using that large hand with cigarette-stained fingernails to turn Riley toward him. I am saying Brother Man stopped Riley on the street, singled him out in front of people dressed, respectively, as Princess Mononoke[28], Storm[29], Daleks[30], Cybermen[31], and Neil deGrasse Tyson[32] (both in blackface and in their own black faces), put his hands on him, and forced him to look into Brother Man's own face with the familiarity of a friend yet, contextually, with the violence of a stranger.

On any other day Riley might have acknowledged that he was wrong to walk past Brother Man's initial "Howyoudoin," which he pretended not to hear on account of the Fetty. On this day, however, Riley felt that since he was inhabiting the character of Tamaki, his decision to ignore Brother Man was just right, an exercise in method acting.

Riley was more than surprised — and did not need to borrow Tamaki's affectations to feel slighted — that Brother Man had touched him, and by that point, even though he might have been just the kind of buyer for what Brother Man was selling, his pride wouldn't let him concede[33].

• • •

It had long irked[34] Riley that his blackness or the degree of his loyalty to the cause should be suspect because he wore blue contacts and bleached his hair blond and because, on top of all that, his name was also Riley, and not, say, Tyreke. It irked him that he might be mistaken for a self-hating Uncle Tom because he enjoyed cosplay and anime and comic book conventions and because he happened to be feeling the character of a rich Japanese schoolboy a little too much at that very moment.

By the time Brother Man said, "Uppity[35], gay-looking nigga," Riley had bypassed logic and forgotten that he held none of the privileges of his costume.

There ensued then what Riley, in his costume, might have called fisticuffs[36], though in everyday life he would have simply said they got to scrappin[37], right on Figueroa Street.

The people who watched and filmed and circulated the scene from inside one of the lobbies of the convention center said it was just like Naruto v. Pain, only with two black guys, so you couldn't tell if either one was the hero.

2.

In truth Brother Man was burly[38] but not violent and rather liked to regard himself as an intellectual in a misleading package. If he could have made a wish before the end of that day, it would have been that he, too, had worn a costume to soften the effects of his image.

When he put his hand on Riley's shoulder, it was only because he disliked the sight of someone, especially one of his own, turning his back to him without hearing him out. It was also because he needed to promote *Brother's Spawn* and had thus far convinced a meager[39] four passersby to buy a $4 copy that day, and because Brother Man felt, unapologetically[40], that black people should stick together and that the blue-eyed, wig-wearing brother in the purple suit should have at least acknowledged him with a nod, if not a handshake or a howyoudoin.

Though in the aftermath, people would call his papers religious tracts, indoctrination[41] materials, and "some kind of gang documents," *Brother's Spawn* was Brother Man's self-published dystopian[42] comic series set at Pasadena City College[43], where he first learned of Octavia Butler[44] and her work. The comics were hand-drawn with the dimensions of a postcard, though he also hoped to sell broadsides featuring a poem he had written. Brother Man — aliases[45] Kyle Barker, Cole Brown, Overton Wakefield Jones, Tommy Strawn, and pen name

[27] to **accost** = to stop somebody and speak to them in a rude or threatening way
[28] **Princess Mononoke** = a main character of a 1997 Japanese animated epic historical fantasy film
[29] **Storm** = a fictional character from American comic books
[30] **Daleks** = a fictional extraterrestrial race of mutants in the British science-fiction TV series *Doctor Who*
[31] **Cybermen** = a fictional race of cyborgs in the British science-fiction TV series *Doctor Who*
[32] **Neil deGrasse Tyson** = an American astrophysicist, planetary scientist and author
[33] to **concede** = to admit (often unwillingly)
[34] to **irk** = to irritate or annoy
[35] **uppity** = (informal) haughty or snobbish
[36] **fisticuffs** = a not very impressive fight
[37] **scrappin'** = fighting (without the intention of causing serious pain)
[38] **burly** = having a broad body and strong muscles
[39] **meager** = very little, not enough
[40] **unapologetic** = without feeling sorry or expressing regret
[41] **indoctrination** = the process of teaching someone a particular belief so that they accept it uncritically and reject other beliefs
[42] **dystopian** = an imagined world or society in which life is characterized by fear and the loss of freedom and individuality
[43] **Pasadena City College** = a public community college in the city of Pasadena
[44] **Octavia E. Butler** (1947–2006) was an American science-fiction author.
[45] **alias** = another (false) name someone uses

Brother Hotep — was selling the postcard comics illegally (he preferred the term "without official city permits") between a food truck and a juice cart that day. On other days he sold them near the Century City Mall, in Ladera Heights[46], in Little Ethiopia[47], and as far as Inglewood[48].

That day, he banked on the convention center's Comic-Love traffic and the potential readers it might attract, boasting to his girlfriend earlier in the morning that he would probably sell out, "even without one of those official tables in the convention center, watch."

And though he would say he was not usually the type to call Riley a sellout[49] or an Uncle Tom[50], that day, Brother Man (real name Richard Simmons, yes, Richard Simmons) could not handle Riley's refusal to acknowledge him or his art. He could find reasons to dismiss the hundred or so people in costumes, some speaking English, some other languages, who shook their hands no at the laminated mock-ups he tried to show them, but he could not abide a black refusal, especially one from a black guy in a Japanese prep-schoolboy costume, the very kind of audience Brother Man hoped to cultivate.

Thus, when he put his hand on Riley's shoulder, he never meant to hit him, and if he could, Brother Man, hereafter Richard, would have imagined that Riley didn't plan to fight him either. And neither man ever would have thought that amateur karate (pronounced in the authentic Japanese accent) would be involved, their arms flailing and legs kicking out in poorly choreographed mortal combat.

3.

On his way to a meeting, Kevan stopped at the SweetArt Bakeshop in Saint Louis to purchase a vegan brownie for himself and a purple cupcake with tiny candy hearts for his daughter Penny, who was with him for the weekend. The whole shop was lined with canvases of varying sizes, painted by the owners and sold from the bakery, which served as a gallery and community meeting space. Tiny vases holding local flowers adorned each table. Kevan wore a black T-shirt that said in white letters, "Eff Your Respectability Politics." He liked the irony of the word "eff" instead of the F-word, but he still debated whether it was better to change "your" to "yo." He wasn't sure if anyone understood the stakes in these decisions or in any of his other art, which he sold online, from his car, and occasionally from a small suitcase in the barbershop on Washington Avenue.

He had one hour left with Penny before her mother would pick her up so Kevan could meet a potential business partner and pitch an idea that he couldn't shake. He chose a table in the middle of the nearly empty shop, with yellow-and-green flowers in the vase. "She's a superhero," Penny said, pointing to the largest canvas on the wall adjacent to the bakery case, and inhaling another glob of frosting. The frosting accumulated at the corners of Penny's smile, but her tongue missed those spots each time it swept her mouth.

"She's cute. Daddy can teach you to paint like this," Kevan said, passing Penny a napkin across the table.

Kevan wasn't a vegan, but he supported black business and black art, and regarded SweetArt as a place where his own work might one day be represented. The T-shirt sales provided him a stash[51] of petty cash, but Kevan had sold only three paintings, and that grieved him. He supported his daughter Penny with a court order and a "real job" as a UPS deliveryman, but he "always took care of my responsibilities," even before Penny's mother, whom he alternately called a gold digger[52], that whore, and my queen, demanded official monthly payments.

"My superhero name is gonna be" — Penny paused to pull back the wrapper and expose the last quarter of the cupcake, its frosting smooshed and all the candy hearts gone — "my name's gonna be Purple. Purple Penny Powers. I will make things purple like this," Penny said, zapping something with her arm.

"Purple Penny Powers." Kevan pretended this was cuter than it was. "Wow."

He was trying not to think about a joke he had seen earlier in the day, trying not to remember the sight of two dead bodies that had appeared casually in his news feed, trying to rehearse instead his pitch for the realization of something he had read in a book that he found in a used bookstore.

The Afric-American Picture Gallery was a series of written sketches by William Wilson, under the pen name Ethiop and following the form of similar sketches — which Kevan found with more research — by James McCune Smith in *The Heads of the Colored People* and Jane Rustic (a.k.a. Frances Ellen Watkins Harper, a black abolitionist[53] poet and suffragist[54]). Kevan wanted to commission painters, including mostly himself, to create a full exhibit of heads of the colored people, now and then, to take the written,

Annotations

[46] **Ladera Heights** = an area in Los Angeles County, California
[47] **Little Ethiopia** = a neighborhood in Los Angeles, California
[48] **Inglewood** = a city in the Los Angeles metropolitan area
[49] **sellout** = somebody who is considered to have done something which used to be against their principles
[50] **Uncle Tom** is the main character of Harriet Beecher Stowe's novel *Uncle Tom's Cabin* (1852). Here the name refers to a person regarded as very subservient, thus betraying their ethnic and cultural community.
[51] **stash** = a secret store of something
[52] **gold digger** = here: a woman who strives to marry a wealthy man
[53] **abolitionist** = a person who is in favour of the end of slavery
[54] **suffragist** = a person who is in favour of women having the right to vote

literary work and render it visually. The idea intrigued him, the heads talking to him like the books in Equiano[55] — though he didn't know that reference yet.

In Kevan's collection, there would be, as in Ethiop's original, Phyllis Wheatley[56], Nat Turner[57], and a doctor, but he would update his favorite sketch, "Picture 26," of the "colored youth" who was "surrounded by abject wretchedness[58]" to reflect a sort of current abjection. To these he would add a superhero for Penny and a collage of the black men (and women, he would concede, with some coaxing[59] later from Paris Larkin) who had been killed by police and other brutalities.

"Now what's your name going to be?" Penny's voice seemed especially shrill at the moment.

"I don't know." Kevan was still thinking about the bodies and the grainy[60] video of the two men arguing and the way one of the men had held out his hand when the police officer entered the scene; it was clear that the man wasn't holding a gun or a knife, but something soft, like paper.

"Daddy, your name," Penny demanded.

"I don't know," Kevan repeated, and blurted out the first thing that came to his mind: "Bruh Man."

"Bruh Man?" Penny jutted[61] her head back. "What does he do?"

"He paints, and whatever he wishes, he can paint it and make it happen." Kevan made Penny lick a napkin so he could wipe the leftover icing from her face. "And he can make bad things unhappen, if he paints them right."

"That's gonna be my power, too," Penny said, pulling away from his grooming and hesitating in the way of five-year-olds, "but I'm just gonna think and make it happen or unhappen."

He wished briefly that things were so simple and then began to outline something on a napkin.

4.

Paris Larkin was meeting Riley at the convention center after two shifts at her part-time job for Dark Shadows Hollywood Cemetery Tours. Her official job description said, "Tour Narrator: Vocal talent. Must be able to memorize stories and stand for long periods of time on moving bus while engaging audiences." I ain't saying she a gravedigger, Riley liked to begin when he introduced her as his girlfriend, but really, she digs graves, like, loves them. It was one of the things that had attracted him to her when they first met, her dark cheeriness and her nonjudgmental approach to his lifestyle. And his soft-landing punch lines were one of the things Paris liked about him, and his interesting face, and the way he wasn't at all who she expected him to be.

When he took his contact lenses out at night and tied his hair down with a durag[62], Riley looked just as comfortable and kind as when he dressed up and hung out at his favorite comic café in Pasadena, drinking boba tea[63] and playing chess with kids from Caltech[64], where he studied engineering and was one of a handful of black students on campus.

If Paris could have a superpower, it would be to make herself visible, because even though she stood at the front of the bus with a microphone, pointing out alleged sightings of Marilyn Monroe to hungry tourists with camera phones and fake Gucci sunglasses, she wasn't the main attraction, and she preferred to narrate the tours with reverence[65] instead of theatrics, to fade into the background and let the spirits speak for themselves. With Riley she could be seen, since they got a decent amount of attention when they were together and especially when they dressed up. Certain cosplay purists (read: racists) did not always approve of Paris's or Riley's respective costume choices or the idea of black people dressed as nonblack characters. Paris had come to anticipate and almost enjoy the surge[66] of anxiety that came with entering these spaces, had felt her flight-or-fight instinct the closest thing to being fully alive. And the ghost tours, too, made her think that by comparison, she was at least more alive than the bodies that filled those holes.

That day was not her day off, so she took the Metro and two buses to meet Riley at the convention after work, after showering and changing into her long silver wig and meticulously[67] sewn necromancer[68] dress, her dark skin contrasting with the purple-and-white pinstripes of the dress, the gray armor on her arms and legs elevating

[55] **Olaudah Equiano** was a writer and abolitionist in the 18th century. As a child, he was enslaved in Africa and taken to the Caribbean. He purchased his freedom in 1766. Later he went to London, where he supported the abolitionist movement.
[56] **Phyllis Wheatley** was an African-American author in the 18th century. As a child, she was sold into slavery and taken to North America. She learned to read and write and became the first African-American author whose poetry was published.
[57] **Nat Turner** was an enslaved preacher who organized a four-day rebellion of enslaved and free African Americans in Southampton County, Virginia, in 1831.
[58] **wretchedness** = the feeling of being ill, very unhappy or unfortunate and suffering greatly
[59] to **coax** = to gently try to persuade someone to do something
[60] **grainy** = looking as if it is made up of lots of spots so that it is difficult to see something
[61] to **jut** = to move a part of your body in a determined way

[62] **durag** = a cloth tied around the hair
[63] **boba tea** = bubble tea
[64] **Caltech** = California Institute of Technology, a private research university in Pasadena, California
[65] **reverence** = a feeling of great respect for someone or something
[66] **surge** = a sudden powerful movement
[67] **meticulous** = very careful
[68] **necromancer** = someone who claims to be able to communicate with the dead

her mood. She had debated dressing as Haruhi Fujioka[69], the counterpart to Riley's costume from *Ouran High School Host Club*, but her choice of Eucliwood Hellscythe[70] created a bigger impact, she thought. Though she kept her blue contacts down and focused on her sketchbook, her eyelids, adorned with heavy black-and-white shadow, warned other transit passengers to dare her, that day.

When Paris entertained visitors from out of town, or when she and Riley caught the spirit, she liked to ride the Metrolink from Highland Park to Glendale to visit Michael Jackson's mausoleum, which you couldn't exactly get close to, but which still sent a melancholy shiver through her and her guests. During most of her time on the bus or the Metrolink, Paris drew Riley and many other people – you could call her a sketch artist, though not in any official, paying capacity.

She called her sketchbooks a collection of heads, for she never drew bodies, and anyway, Paris was lighthearted and laughed frequently, showing the gap between her teeth, not nearly as morbid as her job and curated[71] heads make her sound. She called Riley Fuzzy Lumpkins[72], and he called her Bubbles[73]. She was listening to "Say My Name,"[74] attached as she was to all things nineties, even though she was nineteen and had been born after Tupac[75] and Biggie[76] were already dead. That morning, Paris had watched reruns of *Martin*[77] and laughed at a character's plea for a wish sandwich. In the nineties, she felt – and you should fill in for yourself a kind of longing here – something melancholy, plaid, flannel, but not overwrought[78].

It isn't true, at least not in Paris's case, that you can sense what the future holds. That day, she had jokingly, in an exercise of character acting, avoided pronouncing Riley's name near the word "death" or at the graveyard or while dressed as Eucliwood, lest she kill him. But no psychic, metaphysical force warned her to tell Riley not to go to Comic-Love or to avoid arguments without spoils or to immediately put his hands up when instructed to do so. Nothing told her, still humming "Say My Name" in her best humming voice, not to walk toward the large crowd of flashing lights, police cars, and costumed and uncostumed bystanders. Her stomach urged her to look away, once she got close enough to be sickened, but she couldn't then.

She didn't feel more alive from the surge of panic in her body or in comparison to Riley on the ground.

Years later, she would regret not drawing the offending officer that day. Since then, she has sketched his face over and over, penciling his name and image in her notebook as a sort of plea, saying it aloud, wishing that she, like Eucliwood, could pronounce the names of those she wanted to die and make it so.

When an artist named Kevan Peterson wrote to her about a project he wanted to finish – really, to finally begin – Paris was glad for her sketches of Riley.

5.

A well-read, self-aware, self-loving black man with blue contact lenses and blond hair and a periwinkle suit was shot down in Los Angeles after a reportedly violent altercation[79] with a well-read street promoter, who was also shot, after police officers answered a complaint. "Who was also shot" here signals the afterthought that was Brother Man, Richard, because he was not the one with the blond hair or blue contacts or in any way exceptional, except for his size and the things he had overcome (too many to name here), and his comic books. And you should fill in for yourself the details of that shooting as long as the constants (unarmed men, excessive force, another dead body, another dead body) are included in those details. Hum a few bars[80] of "Say My Name," but in third person plural if that does something for you.

A few more points I should not leave to the imagination: in the chalk drawing on Fifteenth, you can see Riley's leg kicking out like Spike Spiegel[81] and an additional rectangle above the outline of Richard's hand, where he might have held his comic books or a laminated mock-up.

The picture the Associated Press chose came from a Throwback Thursday photo that Riley had posted on social media, a picture of him in a costume from an undergrad party, at which he wore an oversize blue shirt and a bedazzled[82] blue bandana over cornrows. His mother, and girlfriend, Paris, explained repeatedly that he was not dressed as a thug[83], but as nineties Justin Timberlake.

Annotations

[69] **Haruhi Fujioka** = the main character of the manga and anime series *Ouran High School Host Club*
[70] **Eucliwood Hellscythe** = a main character of *Is This a Zombie?*, a Japanese light novel series
[71] **curated** = organized and presented professionally
[72] **Fuzzy Lumpkins** = a villain in *The Powerpuff Girls*, an American superhero animated TV series
[73] **Bubbles** = a main character of *The Powerpuff Girls*
[74] **"Say My Name"** = a song released in 1999 by the American girl group Destiny's Child
[75] **2Pac** = Tupac Amaru Shakur (1971–1996) was an American rapper and actor.
[76] **Biggie** = Christopher George Latore Wallace (1972–1997) was an American rapper and songwriter.
[77] ***Martin*** = an American TV sitcom (1992–1997)
[78] **overwrought** = extremely excited or upset and worried

[79] **altercation** = a noisy argument or fight
[80] **bar** = one of the small equal parts into which a piece of music is divided
[81] **Spike Spiegel** = the main character of the 1998 anime series *Cowboy Bebop*
[82] **bedazzled** = sparkly
[83] **thug** = a violent person or criminal

Brother Man's picture was an old mug shot, accompanied by a story that emphasized a criminal charge from five years ago — for child support nonpayment and tax evasion — and his penchant[84] for false names.

Both men's families would say the pictures didn't say anything, that that's not how anyone who knew them would remember them.

The Neil deGrasse Tysons disagreed over the number of gunshots they heard; the one in blackface said ten, while the one with a brown face called black said thirteen. The autopsies would not conclude, but there might have been marijuana in Riley's or Richard's systems, at some point.

6.

I think a cop shooting is too melodramatic when the story was interesting on its own, and my preoccupation with race is perhaps overdone, but it was O'Connor, I think, who said — and I say "I think" here more as a device, to affect a sort of nonchalance, when in fact I know she said — everything that rises must converge or something like that ("or something like that" serving as another affected clause). But that makes the ending sound intentional or overdetermined, when it wasn't, though I believe — I know — it was Donika Kelly[85] who said "the way a body makes a road," or in this case an outline, impression.

How to end such a story, especially one that is this angry, like a big black fist? The voice is off-putting. All the important action happens offscreen; we don't even see the shooting or the actual bodies or the video. Like that one guy in fiction workshop said, meta is so eighties. The *mise en abyme*[86] is cool but overdone. This is a story of fragments, sketches. Dear author: Thank you for sharing this, but we regret.

I concede that it might have been so much more readable as a gentle network narrative, with the cupcakes and the superheroes and the blue eyes and the nineties image-patterning. But I couldn't draw the bodies while the heads talked over me, and the mosaic formed in blood, and what is a sketch but a chalk outline done in pencil or words? And what is a black network narrative but the story of one degree of separation, of sketching the same pain over and over, wading through so much flesh trying to draw new conclusions, knowing that wishing would not make them so?

• • •

[84] **penchant** = a special liking for something
[85] **Donika Kelly** = an Assistant Professor of English at the University of Iowa, specializing in poetry writing and gender studies in contemporary American literature
[86] ***mise en abyme*** = a formal technique of creating an image that contains a smaller copy of itself

WHILE READING

3

Read the short story. Match the sentence parts. Write the letters A–E in the boxes.

1 Riley and Paris often hang around the town ☐

2 On his way to the Convention Center, where he is meeting Paris, Riley ignores Brother Man's greeting ☐

3 Not being pleased about Riley's lack of interest, Brother Man ☐

4 The confrontation between Riley and Brother Man leads to a fight ☐

5 Both Brother Man and Riley are shot although ☐

A violates Riley's personal space by turning Riley toward him.

B wearing costumes as characters from manga and anime series.

C ending with police intervention.

D being unarmed.

E brushing away the pamphlet Brother Man was trying to hand him.

4

a) Divide the story up into different parts and sum up what happens in each part in no more than four sentences.

b) **Group work**
Compare the structure you came up with and your summaries with your group.

5 Group work

a) Read the short story again. Work in a group of four. Each of you chooses one of the following characters. Note down what you have learned about them and provide references from the text.

b) Present your results to your group members and add the missing information.

Character	Personal information	Outer appearance	Beliefs and values	Relationship to other people	Text reference
Riley					
Brother Man					
Kevan					
Paris					

6 → **Workshop:** Analysing narrative perspective

Analyse the narrative perspective of the short story. How does it challenge the reader's perceptions of the story and its characters?

7

a) Several important African-American personalities are mentioned in the short story. Do some research on:
- Frederick Douglass (l. 46)
- Uncle Tom (ll. 103 and 155)
- William Wilson and *The Afric-American Picture Gallery* (ll. 225–226)
- James McCune Smith and *The Heads of the Colored People* (ll. 228–229)
- Jane Rustic a.k.a. Frances Ellen Watkins Harper (ll. 229–230)

b) Present your findings in class. Speculate on why the narrator mentions these people and their work.

POST-READING

8 Think-Pair-Share

a) **Think:** Make a list of three themes you consider central to your understanding of the short story.
b) **Pair:** Explain your choices to your partner and agree on two major themes.
c) **Share:** Discuss your results in class. Give reasons for your choices by presenting examples from the short story.

9 → **Workshop:** Analysing characters

Compare Riley and Brother Man: What similarities are there between them? How are they different? What separates them?

10 Pair work

Discuss which "apology" the title of the short story refers to.

11

Go back to your assumptions from task 1 and 2 (p. 29).
a) How was the story different from your predictions?
b) Which character stood out the most to you and why?

12

The narrator portrays Brother Man as follows:

"In truth Brother Man was burly but not violent and rather liked to regard himself as an intellectual in a misleading package. If he could have made a wish before the end of that day, it would have been that he, too, had worn a costume to soften the effects of his image." (ll. 118–122)

Explain what this reveals about Brother Man.

13

Comment on the ending of the short story.

14

Analyse the significance of the title of the short story.

15

Read three comments on Nafissa Thompson-Spires's story from an online forum of a reading group.

Anonymous *March 26, 2021 at 4:43 PM*
I was very interested in how the author was able to weave these narratives together but the moment that stood out to me the most was the reality they were able to combine with the creativity in order to send a message. Specifically when it came to Riley and Brother Man, though both did not fit the typical definition of a black man brought on by society as well as our people they were still gunned down like a typical black man. The message I received from this being that black society, as well as general society, needs to cultivate this type of creativity from our black men. So that others can view this creativity as a natural pathway from the harmful rhetoric of not being a typical black man. Not to say that being a typical black man is bad but that younger generations know that they do not have to be made to feel weird for expressing themselves in different ways.

Danielle Hawthorne *March 26, 2021 at 6:19 PM*
Nafissa Thompson-Spires is a unique story teller. Usually in novels, American Americans don't have this much variety. The characters were all unique and different aside from the fact that they are African American. I think this is a very important read because it emphasizes that people in one race are not all the same.

It is kind of breaking that stereotype people have about race. For example a black man with blue eyes was introduced in this section of the book. The author stated that they were his real eyes but people may stereotype and think they are fake just because this is uncommon. At the end of the day same race or not, we are individuals and can express ourselves as such. I enjoyed this section of the book.

Phoenix Johnson *March 25, 2021 at 7:05 PM*
Thompson-Spires has a special writing style in this particular sequencing by showing how 4 people are different in personality and in life, but could still fall to a same fate. Each character has a personality or style that doesn't fit the stereotypes that come with their race. Though in society every one of those four could die because of their skin. At the end of the day the author shows how these four different lives can come together and be connected in a way because of discrimination to their race.

a) **Pair work**
Discuss whether (or not) you agree with each post. Give reasons for your answers.
b) Write your own short comment on the short story.
c) Present your comment in class.

16
Find an alternative ending to the story. Include information the narrator deliberately left out.

17 **Group work**
Write a film script based on the short story. Answer the following questions to prepare the film script.
- What would the setting look like?
- What would the actors look like? Which actors would you employ for the film? Why?
- Which sentences from the short story would you keep to be acted out? What would you change? Why?
- Would you alter the ending of the story? Why (not)?

Mambo Sauce – A short story (2018)

PRE-READING

1 → **S15:** How to describe pictures
Describe the photo below. Use the picture to speculate on the content of the short story and the topics it might be dealing with. The phrases in the box on the right may help you.

Language support

The story might revolve around ...
I expect a story about ...
It's most likely a story about ...
I would imagine that the story's main theme is ...
I think the story/characters ...

2

Initially, read only the first paragraphs of the story (ll. 1–30).

a) **Think:** Characterize the couple's relationship on the basis of this extract. Choose adjectives from the box to describe the couple and their relationship. Add at least two more adjectives.

> loving | balanced | serious | strong | reciprocal | meaningful | harmonious | special | stable | romantic | complex | difficult | ...

b) **Pair:** Share your results with a partner. Decide on three adjectives that you think describe their relationship best.

c) **Share:** In class, discuss reasons why the narrator introduces the couple in this specific way.

Mambo Sauce

by Camille Acker

He had good bones, the archways[1] of his arms when he hugged her, the strong lines of his frame. Constance met him at a bar in Brooklyn. Brian wasn't who she had been looking for, in a place she didn't frequent. A black woman in a mostly white bar talking to a white guy over white music she didn't know. She marveled[2] at his views nonetheless, the intellectual skyline dotted with feminism, prison reform, and progressive economic policy. The negotiations that night took so long she began to wonder if she were making a mistake. He wanted to go out Friday night. She thought Friday was too large a commitment to make. She argued for Sunday brunch. He countered with Saturday night. She held firm: Sunday brunch. Final offer. They shook on it, and when she tried to pull away he held on to her hand and she remembered the good bones, the sturdiness[3] missing from the lean-to[4] men she had dated before.

He became hers. She owned him outright, paid in full. He said so in the midst of a weekend sleepover.

"I should post a sign," he told her, his finger tracing the lines of a rectangle on the left side of his chest. "Property of Constance."

"Is this what you expected?" she said.

"You're what I've been looking for."

"Exactly?" she asked. She had seen pictures of his ex-girlfriends. He had dated black women before, he told her that first night. Dated black women before, sure, but he had never had a black girlfriend – that word so precious it had been like a child asking for a toy when he first used it to introduce her to a friend.

"Yes. Exactly."

Ownership had been her lifelong dream, not that he didn't require some improvements, the rickety[5] way he told jokes and the creak of a man who at thirty-five strummed a guitar and told stories about the band he had always wanted to start. He got a new job in DC as a charter-school[6] lobbyist and asked if she would come with him. It had only been six months, but Constance surveyed their landscape, even the rockiness of their interracial terrain, took in the height of their possibilities, and said yes. She could always unload him if she decided to move on, but for now, she was invested.

And in DC, Constance could be different. She wouldn't be the part-time teacher and full-time dreamer she had been in New York. She could pursue art, call herself an artist. Brian insisted on it, that she take the time she needed to sculpt and find her voice. Once, Brian had gotten out of bed in the middle of the night, naked and hair tousled, to touch each of the pieces Constance had sculpted. "And what's this one?" he said. "And this?" he asked. He came back to bed and she told him, his face close enough that she could whisper and even then, she felt that if she hadn't spoken the words he would have heard them anyway. She told him about her first sculptures and what impossible work it was until what was once only in her mind formed itself in the world. "You form it," he'd said. He listened and then asked questions, his eyes closing when he did, searching for the right phrase. And one time with his eyes closed, she had mouthed *love* when it was much too early to think such a word, much less press lips, even soundless ones, into forming it. Now, they said that word to each other all the time. Him, first. Him, most often.

★★★

Annotations

[1] **archway** = a passage or an entrance with a curved roof
[2] **to marvel** = to show great surprise, wonder or admiration
[3] **sturdiness** = physical strength
[4] **lean-to** = a small building which is attached to one side of a larger building
[5] **rickety** = shabby, of low quality or in bad condition
[6] **charter school** = a school in the US which is paid for with public money and operated by private organizations

The broker[7] took them all over DC, but the neighborhoods where they really wanted to live – Adams Morgan, Dupont Circle, Shaw – were all out of their price range. Brian had gone to Georgetown but told Constance from the beginning that wasn't the neighborhood for them. They finally found an apartment in Far Northeast, the broker assuring them that the neighborhood was up-and-coming.

"I haven't seen many white people," Constance told Brian after their first visit to the place.

Brian said only, "This place gets so much light." He fingered the old window casements in the apartment and smiled.

The second time she brought it up, over Ethiopian food in Shaw, she asked, "And you'll be comfortable there?"

"My king bed won't fit, but that thing's old anyway and your queen is enough space for us." Brian tore off more injera[8]; he scooped up some of the doro wat[9] with the spongy bread. He swallowed the mouthful and after he sucked on each food-stained finger, he smiled.

The third time, she finally said it outright because she had to be sure. "We're the only interracial couple in the neighborhood," she said.

He laughed. "Connie, how many couples have you seen? The neighborhood is changing. I'm sure we won't be the only ones." Constance was unconvinced. Brian moved toward her, stroking her close-cropped hair. "And so what if we were?"

They moved in the next week. Her parents sent a gift card to help them decorate their new home and promises of coming to visit from California. Her mother had been surprised by Constance's worry about dating a white guy. Her mother was more surprised to discover she hadn't dated one before.

"I always kind of thought that was you," she had told Constance. She yelled to Constance's father just then, a *what* that was impatient and harsh. "I'll have to call you later," her mother said before hanging up and before Constance could ask what her mother had seen in her. She liked living in New York because she could find mixed crowds and parties where she didn't have to skillfully work her body to the ground like other black women could. As a girl in San Francisco, she hadn't learned to do that. Rock and pop had been the soundtrack to her teenage years, when she was just as likely to sing into the hairbrush of her Chinese American best friend as the hair pick of her black one.

Brian's mother – his father dead since he was a teenager – sent love and a hundred-dollar bill in a card from Virginia. She wrote inside, *You'll get the real money when I can call Connie my daughter-in-law.* Brian laughed.

"How long should I tell her that will take?" he asked Constance. She was hanging their curtains.

"Is that at the right height?" she asked, but before he could answer, the rod[10] fell to the floor, heavy with its own weight.

★★★

The first day of Brian's job, Constance began sculpting not long after he left, eager to have something to show him when he got home. Four hours in and she had progressed little. She wandered a circuitous[11] path through their apartment. Brian had a beat-up[12] car that he'd kept in New York, mostly for major grocery store runs, that she could use. She didn't want to drive. In Brooklyn, she walked all the time. One block became ten and she could peer into the open windows of brownstones or eavesdrop[13] on the closest sidewalk conversation.

She got out of their apartment and onto their block, the silence of this city foreign to her. She turned onto a major street and was the only one walking. People waited at a bus stop, the Metro wasn't close. Brian biked the distance and he must have gotten stares on his route. The blocks of the neighborhood had few businesses: a check-cashing place, a Chinese carryout, a furniture-rental store. Then, across the street, Constance saw a pink-and-white striped awning[14] with script that read *Winging It!*

Inside the chicken joint, the air felt heavy with grease. The paint saturated with it. The floor waxed with it. This was where the neighborhood was at lunchtime on a Monday: crowding together to put in orders for fried chicken and fries. The cost of two wings and fries was laughable, only two dollars and twenty-five cents. The price was once lower, the *$2.25* written on paper that had been taped over the last price. One of the women behind the counter was at least in her forties or fifties, another might have been as young as twenty, and a third woman looked to be in her sixties. Age was always hard to tell with black folk.

People clumped together with no sense of a line, but the women, especially the oldest one, knew who was next, as if an invisible number popped up above their head when the bell above the door announced their arrival. The women would point and ask, "What you want, honey?"

Annotations

[7] **broker** = a person whose job is to buy and sell things for other people
[8] **injera** = a type of flat, thin bread, usually made from fermented teff flour and eaten in Ethiopia and Eritrea
[9] **doro wat** = a spicy Ethiopian chicken stew
[10] **rod** = a long, thin bar made of wood or metal
[11] **circuitous** = long and complicated, not straight or direct
[12] **beat-up** = in bad condition, damaged
[13] to **eavesdrop** = to listen secretly to what someone is saying
[14] **awning** = a cloth or plastic cover attached to a building to provide shelter from the rain or sun

A short and stout[15] light-skinned man tended most of the fryers, setting them down into the bubbling grease. The women lifted them up and drained them. They tonged the freshly fried chicken into checkerboard-patterned[16] baskets and then held one large salt and one large pepper shaker above the food. Some of the customers, mostly men, simply nodded for the seasonings. Others said "Everything," and then the women would reach for a bottle of hot sauce too. Constance stood back, she didn't want to come off as a newcomer. She had hit the tail end of the rush it seemed, and once most of the customers cleared, it was her, one burly man up to his elbows in his meal, an older gentleman sitting on one of the few stools in the small place, and the staff.

"Honey?" one of the women asked. She pointed the same finger at Constance she had at everyone else.

"Three chicken wings and fries." The woman nodded and the fry cook dropped a new basket in.

"Best wings in DC," the older gentleman said to her. He moved the brim of his hat up to wipe sweat from his forehead.

"Smells like it," Constance said back.

"Never been here before?" he asked. He had a cane[17] and he leaned into it to get nearer to her. Constance shook her head. She glanced at the women to make sure that wasn't a problem.

"What you doing over here, honey?" the oldest woman asked. Her voice was sly and soft. She wiped the counter down, but kept her eyes on Constance.

"I just moved here," she said. She had thought *we*, but the sentence came out with an *I*.

"From where? Over in Northwest?" one of the other women, the youngest and chubbiest, asked. She had curls under her hairnet.

"No, from out of the city," she said. The burly[18] man eating his chicken turned with a ketchup-laden fry in his hand.

"Baltimore or something?" the young chubby one kept up with her questions.

"New York," Constance said, and then, "Brooklyn, actually." It felt like it would give her more credibility[19].

"Where Brooklyn at?" the young girl rapped, mimicking the famous hip hop line. She laughed and hit the fry cook in the back. He only grunted.

"That girl got too much energy for her own good," the oldest one said to Constance. Constance smiled at the ease between them.

"Well, it's so nice to see some young, single sisters in the neighborhood," the older gentleman said. He winked at her. The women dissolved into laughter[20]. Their shoulders shook with amusement and their heads shook in disbelief.

"Let me find out Mr. Bruce is in here trying to get himself a young girl," the third woman, who had kept quiet until then, said. She was tall and slight, all angles in her white uniform. Under her hairnet, she had a bun of what looked like fake hair on top of her head. "He got a chance?" the woman asked Constance, trying to get her in on the joke. She was eager to join the sorority[21].

"He might be too much man for me," Constance said. She had wanted a good line that was also a little bawdy[22], and the women loved it. They responded in choruses of elongated[23] "Girl" and then "You ain't never lied."

Mr. Bruce did his part by sitting up taller on his stool and tapping his cane on the scuffed linoleum. The oldest one slowed her laughing enough to raise the fry basket and put Constance's food in a container.

"Everything," Constance said. The woman smiled and nodded her approval, she sprinkled hot sauce on generously.

"You want mambo too?" she asked. Constance didn't know what that was and couldn't be sure if she'd said *mambo* or *mumbo*.

"She from New York, she don't know about mambo sauce," the young one said. She grabbed a couple of small plastic containers full of red sauce from a nearby counter. "Try it." She opened one and offered it to Constance, who dipped a finger in and put it in her mouth. It was sweet and spicy, like duck sauce and hot sauce combined. She wasn't sure she liked it, but the woman offered it again. Constance took another finger full, and liked it better that time. She nodded and grabbed two more containers and put them into a paper bag with her food. Constance reached into her pocket for some cash. She would bet they didn't take cards.

"Go on," the oldest one said. "Welcome to the neighborhood." She pushed the bag toward her.

"No, it's so cheap already. I can't let you do that."

"She said go on," the tall one said.

"Maybe we'll get Mr. Bruce to pay for it. He can't let his new girlfriend starve," the youngest said. They rocked with laughter again. Constance joined in and took her food.

"See you tomorrow," someone said just as she pushed her way through the door.

[15] **stout** = fat or thick and strong
[16] **checkerboard-patterned** = a pattern of squares in alternating colours
[17] **cane** = a long, thin stick used by people to help them walk
[18] **burly** = large and strong
[19] **credibility** = the fact that somebody can be believed or trusted
[20] to **dissolve into laughter** = to suddenly start laughing
[21] **sorority** = sisterhood, a strong feeling of friendship and support among women
[22] **bawdy** = containing humorous references to sex
[23] **elongated** = very long and thin

She thought of ideas to sculpt almost as soon as she got back to the house. She reached for her chisel[24] with chicken grease still on her fingers. After half of the second wing and the huge helping of fries, she couldn't eat anymore. Brian gnawed on the last piece of chicken when he came home that night and told her about his day.

"A lot to be done," he said, biting into some fried skin on the wing tip. "But everyone seems up for it."

Constance told him about walking around the neighborhood, but didn't relay her conversation in Winging It! She said only that the people were nice and that when the wings were hot and just out of the fryer, they were even better.

"What's this?" Brian asked, holding up one of the mambo-sauce containers.

"It's this special DC sauce," Constance said. "Try it."

Brian did, but he made a face after. "I don't get it. It's weird."

"I liked it," she said.

"Well you," he said, putting the small containers back into the fridge, "can have all of it."

★★★

Their first weekend in DC, Brian's old college friends had a welcome dinner for them. Constance found a colorful dress and wore large gold hoop earrings with it. Brian said she looked beautiful, but when they got to the friend's townhouse in Georgetown, Constance felt like she'd come to the wrong party. Everyone else was very casual, cargo shorts or jeans and flip-flops. One of the four women had a dress on, but she was unadorned[25]. The pale pink of the dress was pretty but barely registered between her complexion and light blond hair. They all lived in DC, had ever since they graduated from Georgetown together. A couple were lawyers who went from undergrad to Georgetown Law[26]. There was a teacher, Alissa, who grabbed Constance's hands when Brian said she taught in New York. Someone else worked in government like Brian, and others had corporate jobs that Constance lost track of during the introductions. They all knew a lot about politics and world events, and made witty[27] and obscure pop culture references some of her Brooklyn girlfriends wouldn't have caught. But the room didn't roll with laughter and Constance noticed early on that there was no music. She was used to get-togethers that ended in old-school Michael Jackson and hip hop that started with, "Six minutes, six minutes, six minutes, Doug E. Fresh, you're on." The home began to empty out, many of the friends saying their good-nights, until it was just Constance and Brian, and Alissa and her husband, Mark.

"You teach, is that right, Connie?" Mark asked. She would have preferred he call her Constance.

"No, she's a sculptor," Brian said. He turned to Constance and she nodded in approval. "Sculptress?"

"I'm a sculptor," she said, smiling at Alissa instead of Mark.

"Does that get lonely? Just you in the apartment, right?" Alissa asked.

"Oh, she gets out sometimes," Brian said. "Connie brought home this chicken, like the best chicken I've ever had. But then she tries to get me to try this stuff called, wait what is it?" Brian said. He had his hand around a bottle of beer, the other on Constance's knee.

"Mambo sauce," she said, wishing he hadn't brought it up.

"Oh yeah, we call it ghetto sauce," Alissa said. She laughed and the men joined. Constance strained a smile.

"They all talk about it like it's foie gras or something. You don't remember it from college, Bri?" Mark asked. Brian shook his head.

"And where are you guys again?" Alissa asked. "U Street and that area?"

"No. Far Northeast," Brian said.

"God, no idea where that is at all," Alissa said. She turned to Mark for his recognition, but he had none to offer her. "We're so Northwest-bound."

"Well, your part of Capitol Hill[28] is Northeast. And H Street[29] is," Mark offered, parsing[30] the sections of the city.

"And I hear Southwest has really been transforming," Alissa said. Mark nodded.

"We like it over there," Brian said. He squeezed Constance's hand and she limply squeezed his back.

"And it's safe?" Alissa asked. Constance wondered if she had ever even been to the other side of the city.

"Of course," Constance said.

"Any other restaurants besides the fried-chicken place?" Mark asked.

"Lots," Brian said. "The two Chinese carryouts." His friends collapsed in laughter. It was a joke Constance had made to Brian after their first week in the apartment, the place filled with too many boxes to think about cooking and their options limited to chicken wings or shrimp

Annotations

[24] **chisel** = a tool for cutting and shaping wood and stone
[25] **unadorned** = with little or no decoration
[26] **Georgetown Law** = the law school of Georgetown University in Washington, D.C.
[27] **witty** = clever and amusing
[28] **Capitol Hill** = a large neighborhood in Washington, D.C.
[29] **H Street** = the main commercial strip of the Near Northeast neighborhood in Washington, D.C.
[30] to **parse** = to examine something carefully

fried rice. The comparisons to their former hip Brooklyn neighborhoods had run roughshod[31] over Far Northeast.

"And I'm sure the liquor store has a fine collection of 40s[32] to choose from," Alissa said.

"Not every neighborhood needs to be Georgetown," Constance said. "Places like this are so," she searched for the right intellectually damning word, "stagnant. I wouldn't choose a place to live just so I could get an ego boost when I told people." Alissa reddened, her face now a better contrast to her pale pink dress.

"I thought that was the only reason people ever moved to New York," Mark said. He took a sip of his beer, but watched Constance over the bottle's rim.

"Well, that's not why I moved there," Constance said. Brian's fingers tapped out a fevered rhythm on her knee.

"People do lots of things for the reaction they get, right?" Mark looked at Constance and Brian's interlocked hands.

"Like that trick we played on Sigma Chi[33]?" Brian said, moving his hand off Constance's knee to offer Mark a high five. Mark pointed a finger at Brian and began laughing.

"Oh man, and your face when we almost got caught." They began to talk over each other to tell the story and Alissa stiffly asked Constance if she wanted anything else.

★★★

Constance endured another half an hour until finally Brian seemed ready to leave. They said their goodbyes, but Constance held her face away from Mark when he tried to give her a kiss on the cheek. Alissa told Constance she hoped they would see her again soon, but when she said it she looked as if something sharp and sour were contained in her cheeks.

"They're good people," Brian said, when they were in the car and on their way back home.

"I'm sure they are," Constance said.

"Then what was with the Georgetown takedown?" he asked. He pulled up to a red light and turned to face her.

"What about their takedown? And why did you tell them about mambo sauce?" she asked.

"What? They already knew about mambo sauce," he said. The light turned and Brian accelerated, the car jolting forward.

"No, why did you tell them about any of it? The chicken place, my joke about the Chinese carryouts?" she asked. He was driving too fast.

"Why did I make conversation? When clearly you weren't going to?"

"Is this the way we came?" she asked. She peered out at water, but she hadn't remembered any on the way there.

"They're not New Yorkers, okay? But they're still good people," he said. He made a U-turn[34] right before an oncoming car and the horn of the vehicle blared.

"Why do you keep saying they're good people? Like that makes up for being ignorant. *Ghetto sauce*?" she said, yelling this time.

"She didn't mean anything by it. Everyone says *ghetto*."

"I've never heard you say *ghetto*, Brian."

"Well, I've never heard you be a bitch to my friends," he said. He pulled the car over onto a small side street. "I need to goddamn map us back to Northeast."

"I wasn't a bitch. Don't you call me a bitch. You shared something you shouldn't have," she said. "And your friends said things they shouldn't have. Neither of those make me a bitch."

Brian tapped the screen of his phone, his face set aglow with its light and his anger.

"It doesn't even know the address." He typed on his phone, then struck[35] the screen, then banged it on the steering wheel. "We can't even get to the fucking neighborhood, but you want to defend it rather than, for just one night, being nice to my friends?"

"It isn't just one night," Constance said. She turned to look out the window, the lawn of a house before her, a tricycle abandoned until morning. Silence set in.

"No, it isn't. It's a lot of fucking nights," he said. He breathed out. He touched the side of her face, his fingertips on her cheek. "Of us."

Constance hadn't been talking about them. She had been talking about the anger at his friends' ignorance, the lopsidedness[36] of feeling defensive and never knowing when someone was coming to knock her sideways. She had said something about their dismissal of Far Northeast, but had smiled at ghetto sauce. She hadn't bothered to defend loving Brian, to question the look Mark had given. It wasn't just one night of excising the parts of her that didn't create the right picture, a paper doll with cutouts in the right places so that when she was strung up, over archways and doorframes, everyone would be ever so complimentary. It wasn't just one night. Brian was right. It was a lot of fucking nights.

★★★

[31] **roughshod** = completely ignoring
[32] **forty** = a 40-ounce bottle of malt liquor
[33] **Sigma Chi** = one of the largest and oldest all-male college fraternities in the US
[34] **U-turn** = a turn in a half circle to go back in the direction from which you have come
[35] to **strike, struck, struck** = to hit forcefully or violently
[36] **lopsidedness** = the quality of being not equally balanced

Constance's second visit to Winging It! was a whole week after the first. She came a little later that day to avoid the rush, and when she walked inside the oldest waitress pointed a finger at her and asked, "Where you been?"

Constance put her hands together as if pleading for forgiveness. "I know. Shame on me."

"See what happen when you give people free food?" It was the first time she heard the fry cook's voice.

"Earl's right," the woman said. Constance, when she had replayed her first visit, named all the ladies in her head after her girlfriends in Brooklyn. The oldest, bossy one was Gina. The young, sweet one was Joy, and the tall and quiet one was Tracy. She hadn't bothered to name the cook, so she subbed in Earl.

"You give someone the best fried chicken they ever laid lips to," Gina said, "and what you get? No visit, no call, no nothing."

Joy shook her head at Constance.

"How about I pay for this meal and the last one to make up for it?" Constance asked.

"Oh, now we need your charity?" Tracy said. They each tried to hold their belligerence[37], but Gina broke first, laughing off her indignation.

"Come on, what you want?"

Constance walked closer to the counter and relaxed. She ordered fish and asked for everything including the mambo sauce. She'd put some on her eggs one morning, dunked a piece of toast in it the next. They joked with Mr. Bruce again, and Constance found out that the burly, silent customer from last time who was there again was Gina's husband.

"He don't like to talk, and I don't like him to," she said. "It's a match, honey."

Constance laughed with the girls, slapping the counter when someone made an extra-funny joke. Mr. Bruce said he liked Constance eating lots of food. He liked a woman with some thickness. The women joked that he'd have to wait a long time to get that with her.

"Twig, is what she is," Tracy said.

"Look who's talking," Constance shot back. Gina and Joy about died. They slapped each other's backs when they weren't howling into each other's shoulders.

"She think she can come in here talking to anybody any way," Tracy said, but she grinned through the condemnation[38]. "Come on, let's see." Tracy came out from behind the counter and put an arm around Constance. "Call it."

"I don't know, think young Miss might win. She got a little more curve on hers," Joy said.

"What about this though?" Tracy turned around, and the women mm-hmmed.

"Now on that back there," Gina said, motioning for Constance to turn around. "Yup, you got her."

"Give me another order," Constance said. Everyone began to laugh, even Gina's husband.

"What do you do, Twig?" Tracy asked.

"I make art. I'm an artist," Constance said, the words dribbling out of her mouth.

"Like what?" Gina asked.

"You take pictures or something?" Joy asked. She posed with a hand on an errant hip and cast her eyes toward the tile floor. She jumped out of the pose just as quick presenting the palms of her hands to the room in a ta-da.

"No pictures," Constance said, laughing at Joy's enthusiasm.

"I don't know if I can sit long enough for a painting, but I could try." Joy hopped back to her pose and froze.

"I sculpt," Constance finally said.

"Like these statues we got all over this city? You might need to move somewhere else, where there's less competition," Gina said.

"You should do a statue for this place," Mr. Bruce said.

"Shoot, she might as well make you a statue, Mr. Bruce. Don't know the last time you weren't sitting on that stool," Tracy said.

"Ain't that the truth. I open up and seem like he's already sitting there. Sleeping upright in here," Gina said. She and Tracy celebrated their tag-team[39] comedy.

"I could do a statue of Mr. Bruce maybe," Constance said, hoping for Gina and Tracy's approval.

"No cane though, better to capture me when I was in my prime."

"Who says you aren't still?" Constance said. Joy began whooping in approval.

"We could see your work somewhere?" Gina asked.

"Probably in New York, one of those museums up there," Joy said.

"No, nowhere like that. Everything is just in the apartment right now," Constance said. At least this time she hadn't used "my apartment." "*The* apartment" betrayed no one.

"What you waiting for?" Tracy asked.

"Well, somebody's gotta want to see it," Constance said.

"You believe in you?" Gina asked. Constance nodded, afraid of chastisement[40] if she shrugged her shoulders or told her maybe. "You got somebody else who believe in you?" Gina asked. Constance nodded, picturing Brian

Annotations

[37] **belligerence** = the state of being hostile or aggressive, the wish to fight or argue

[38] **condemnation** = the act of saying that something is very bad

[39] **tag-team** = people who take turns to do something

[40] **chastisement** = severe criticism

that night in New York, Brian insisting that all she needed was the time to become a great artist. "Then you got everything. You bring one of those in here. We'll make space on the counter or something. Move Mr. Bruce over for a few days."

"That's too sweet of you," Constance said, waving away Gina's offer. She didn't know if they would like her work, if it might strike them as too foreign, as too little, as too much.

"You need something. We can give it to you. No museum in New York, but we can start calling that counter, the Winging It! Gallery. Might as well do it now before we can't anymore."

"What do you mean?" Constance asked. Joy and Tracy's heads were hung a bit and Mr. Bruce lowered the rim of his hat.

"We closing at the end of the month," Gina said.

★★★

Winging It! opened in 1968, Gina told her. She and her silent-type husband had watched DC burn after Martin Luther King's assassination. They didn't live in Shaw, where the most damage was done, but they had both grown up around H Street, which had burned almost entirely that day in April. They wanted to do something and they thought what the city needed was new black businesses, people who could show they believed in the city. They borrowed and begged from whomever they could to open and even bought the building.

"Nobody was thinking about this building, about this neighborhood. Scandal how cheap it was and now, they telling us we can get all kinds of money for it. We said no for a long time, but they get personal. They come in saying, 'Ma'am, you must want to do something else. You must not want to stand in here frying chicken for people. Who would want that?' Like my whole life don't mean a thing."

Developers were looking for areas for new condos[41]. This section was filled with single-family homes, not as easy to rent out to young professionals who wanted shiny new amenities[42] without the hassle[43] of a house. The privilege of ownership.

"You can't close," Constance told her. "What will the neighborhood do?"

"Change come for all of us, honey," Gina said and sent her on her way with three free chicken wings.

But that night, welcoming change wasn't what Constance wanted to do. She ranted to Brian instead.

"More than forty years," she told him, shaking a spatula at him as vegetables sizzled in a skillet. "They started because of the riots. This is how neighborhoods are destroyed."

Brian cracked open a beer and took a seat at the kitchen table. "Well, we should go and support them as much as we can before they close."

Constance nodded, but she didn't want him coming into Winging It! with her. She didn't want them to know that she was with a white guy and that the way she talked when she was with them wasn't the way she talked when she was with him.

"Someone decides that newer is better," she said. "People have no sense of their history. And this developer she's selling to, he's done this all over the city. Put developments in historically black neighborhoods, moved out small businesses." She got two plates down from the cabinet and began to dish up a plate for him. "I'm going to email some people. Maybe the *Washington Post*, the *City Paper*, local stations, tell them the story and see if I can get something to happen." She set his plate in front of him.

"You talked to them about this?" Brian said. He began eating, furrowing his brow as he did. "They want you to stop it?"

"You haven't even been in there," Constance said. She opened a beer for herself and took a long sip. She turned away from him.

"You're right. Maybe I should go in soon."

"Don't go just because I said to go," she said, pressing reprimand[44] into her voice so insistently that he would feel it.

"What? Who said that? And you didn't say I should go, you've never said that."

"The point is, it's a real shame," she said. Constance began to make a plate for herself.

"What's a shame is people burning their own neighborhoods. It's like, why do that?" he said.

"Rage," she said. One of her aunts had witnessed the Watts riots in '65. She had told Constance that all that love had to go somewhere. Constance had asked, "Love?"

"I guess you thought that was hate?" her aunt had said.

"Of course. But in the end, rioting accomplishes nothing." He laid his hands out on the table, open in supplication[45].

"I don't know if protest is always meant to be productive," she said. "Sometimes you just have to get something out of your system."

"Only to destroy yourself?"

★★★

[41] **condo** = condominium, an apartment building in which each apartment is owned by the person who lives in it
[42] **amenity** = something, such as a shopping centre or sports facilities, that is intended to make life more pleasant or comfortable for people
[43] **hassle** = a situation that causes difficulty or trouble
[44] **reprimand** = strong disapproval or criticism
[45] **supplication** = the act of asking a god or someone who is in a position of authority for something in a humble way

Television coverage was more than Constance expected, but the call to the *City Paper* had yielded interest. The reporter there had mentioned a reporter he knew at a local station. That reporter called Constance and said they could do a live remote the next day. Constance put on a bright orange dress, something vivid for the cameras, and got there just before noon.

"Anne won't come out," the reporter said to Constance after a brief hello and handshake. Constance turned to Winging It! and back to the reporter, doused in perfume and the irritation of someone with something better to do.

"Anne?"

"The owner." The reporter began to reek of her indignation. "She says she's running her business and doesn't have time for some news story."

"Well, it is the lunch rush." Inside Winging It!, the crowd was dense, hungry patrons[46] layered over one another. Constance couldn't find Gina/Anne in all of that thickness. "Maybe after, you could talk to her," Constance offered.

"It's a live remote. I told you. You're gonna have to talk."

Constance craned again to see if she could spot Gina. She saw Tracy yelling over her shoulder, probably at Earl for an order. Constance couldn't catch her eye and going inside to talk to one of them felt pointless, casting her voice on too turbulent a sea. "Okay," she said.

Constance dabbed a tissue at her nose and cheekbones, hoping to clear any shine that the camera might catch. The cameraman counted them down to go live. The reporter struck a smile, her teeth shining brightly, and thanked the anchor miles away in the studio. Constance tried to construct sentences in her head to make sure she wouldn't fumble any words, but the reporter's intro was too short and the microphone was in her face too soon.

"And how long have you been coming to Winging It!?" the reporter asked.

"Forever it feels like," Constance said. Two times seemed an infinitesimal[47] number to tell her. "Gina and the girls have made it feel like home." Constance had used her private name, but there was no recovery on live television.

"And what makes the food so good?"

"Well, it's the best fried chicken in the city," Constance parroted Mr. Bruce's pronouncement since she hadn't had fried chicken from anywhere else. "And of course, you have to get it with the mambo sauce."

"And what makes this place important?"

"It's a cornerstone of the community and when we allow developers to come in and take away these cornerstones, the whole structure collapses. This developer has done this all over DC and here's a place where we can take a stand against it. They think they know better than the people of this community what is best for them. We think they're wrong."

The reporter moved the mic away. "The developer has suggested a mixed-use complex, some condos as well as retail. But inside right now, lots of hungry Washingtonians are getting their fill of this institution before it closes. Anna Bruce and her husband, George, started this restaurant in the wake of the riots of 1968, and now this city will be losing a place to all sit down at the table of brotherhood as Dr. King would have said, with some of the best fried chicken in the city in hand."

The cameraman swung toward the door of Winging It! just as Brian exited, a greasy white paper bag in his hands, Gina behind him.

"Back to you."

★★★

Gina had beckoned[48] Constance into Winging It! with just one wave of her hand and one set, stern line of her mouth. Constance asked Brian to wait outside, she wouldn't be long, she said. Brian followed her back inside anyway, as if the words she'd spoken had been no more than her own discarded thought. She tried to stand just a bit apart from Brian. Not that she was denying him or that they were together; she wouldn't do that. She just wanted to handle her own business with Gina, explain that it was like Gina had told her about bringing in a sculpture: they had needed something and Constance had been able to give it.

"Who asked you to do that?" Gina asked. Her hands rushed the air, propelled by anger toward Constance and the sidewalk that the news crew had abandoned only minutes ago. Constance opened her mouth to reply, but stopped. "You know my name?" Gina said. "Or hers?" She pointed at Tracy. "So, how you know what I want?"

"I just thought if you could stay here," Constance's voice began to rise, "it would be better," she said.

"For you?" Gina said. "So you can come in here and chat with women who work for a living?"

"I told you, I sculpt," Constance said quietly.

"And live with your white boyfriend," Gina said. Constance looked around Winging It!, but Mr. Bruce wouldn't meet her eyes and neither would any of the other women. "That's your man, sister?" Gina asked. She pointed her finger at Constance, her ordering finger, the one that gave you permission to ask for what you were willing to pay for, the one that allowed her to give you

Annotations
[46] **patron** = (formal) customer
[47] **infinitesimal** = extremely small

[48] to **beckon** = to signal somebody to come nearer

what you were looking for or tell you that they were all out of that.

"It's been six months," she said. Constance shrank inside, her courage fleeting enough to escape her in one short sneeze.

Gina lowered her finger and shook her head. "You think just because you black, you not changing this neighborhood?" she said. Constance's hand went to her hair, feeling for her blackness. Gina raised her finger again, this time for Brian. "He asked questions. Wanted me to tell him what was the best choice, how he should order, whether people really got salt, pepper, and hot sauce or if that would make it too salty. You came in here like you knew. You never asked anything. You thought you knew better. You thought you *were* better. Just because you live on this side of town don't mean you don't think like they do on the other side of town. Go save a business in Georgetown, honey," she said, punctuating the most important words with her finger. That finger ruled the whole place.

"I was helping."

"You were interfering. I knew who I was selling this place to. Maybe that developer puts a good grocery store in here or a drugstore that doesn't keep its soap under lock and key. I love this place, put my whole life into even the corners of it, but even I know there are better things in this world than two-dollar fried chicken wings." She pointed one red nail to the plateglass window and the gray of the neighborhood beyond it. "But you too busy knowing it all to ever figure out what someone else knows. You so sure of things, how come you didn't know to tell us you didn't move down here alone?" Gina thumbed in Brian's direction. "Now, I gotta hope this developer don't say to me, 'Never mind,' don't say, 'Maybe she's too much trouble to sell to and maybe those Chinese down the street might be easier to deal with.' Now, I gotta make sure that the life I decided I wanted isn't gonna get wrecked by some girl who don't even know what the hell my name is."

Gina slammed a fist onto the counter. She turned and walked through the doors to the back. Constance and the whole room watched her go. Then the others turned to Constance. She headed straight for the door, Brian stood still behind her. His face was filled with the fire that had just been on Gina's. Before she could reach the door, she caught her foot on Mr. Bruce's cane. He didn't give her any of his teasing, none of his innuendo. She was quiet too, begging in silence to just get out of the door. Outside, shame and the smell of grease clung to her.

★★★

Brian eventually came outside and began to walk to their house, in front of Constance. Her feet didn't bother to catch up, unsure of how deep the water was around her and with no insurance to take care of the damage after.

In their apartment, Brian was hushed. The rustle[49] of the bag from Winging It! when he set it down with no gentleness, with no ease, was the loudest of anything.

"Why didn't they know about me?" he asked.

Constance didn't know what answer would be both true and painless. She could find none.

"She made it sound like I was hiding something," she said.

"You never said, 'My boyfriend thinks' or 'My boyfriend says'?"

"I didn't talk to them like that."

"It's only been six months, right?"

"I was helping. I was doing my best."

"People are always lying when they say that."

"You don't understand anything," she said, but tried to bury the words in an exhale.

"Say that again," he said. Constance could not and she still could not look at him.

"No, I understand everything," he said. He walked away from her.

Before long, the apartment began to darken. Constance went into the kitchen, wanting a beer or perhaps nothing at all. The chicken, still in its white bag, sat on the table, cold and neglected[50]. It seemed a shame for it to be wasted, but Constance thought it best to get it out of the house. She would have scrubbed her memory of this afternoon if she could have, at least she could scrub the kitchen of it. She pushed the bag into the trash, ripping it as she did. Mambo sauce tumbled out and when she pushed more, the small plastic containers opened. Dark sauce spilled on its journey to the bottom of the bin. Maybe she had never even liked the taste of mambo sauce. The vinegar too sharp and the sweetness too thick. She hadn't been tasting the sauce as much as she had been tasting newness. That was what those developers wanted.

Gentrification[51] was always good at first: fresher produce at the grocery store, a cleaner subway station. Then, a new shop replaced the family-owned one that had been there for decades. The crumbling row house – an eyesore[52] for its boarded-up windows, but beautiful when the first snow collected in the jagged remnants[53] of its roof – is gone one day to make way for high-rise condos. This is what Brian didn't understand: once gentrification started it could not be stopped. And Constance was afraid love would do the same to her.

[49] **rustle** = a soft, dry sound
[50] **neglected** = not receiving proper attention

[51] **gentrification** = the process by which a part of a city changes from being a poor area to a more expensive place where wealthier people move in
[52] **eyesore** = a very ugly or unpleasant sight
[53] **remnant** = a small part of something that is left from a larger original piece or amount

WHILE READING

3

Read the short story. Then answer the following questions.

a) How did Constance and Brian start dating?

b) How does each of them benefit from moving to DC?

c) What is special about the neighborhood they moved to?

d) How do their parents react to their relocation?

e) What kind of place is Winging It! and who does Constance meet there?

f) What is Constance's reaction to trying mambo sauce? What is Brian's?

g) Why is the atmosphere tense at the welcome dinner Brian's old college friends prepared for them?

h) What is the reason for the dispute Brian and Constance have on their way home?

i) Why is Winging It! closing at the end of the month?

____

____

j) What does Constance do to prevent Winging It! from closing and what is the owner's reaction to it?

____

____

k) How does Brian react to the incident at Wining It! on their way home and in their apartment?

____

____

l) What does the narrator say about "gentrification" at the end of the story?

____

____

4

Read the statements below. Decide whether the statements are true or false. Tick (✓) the correct box. Provide evidence from the text for each statement.

Statement		True	False	Evidence
1	Brian has never had a black girlfriend before.			
2	Brian ignores Constance's comment on the mostly black neighborhood.			
3	Constance tells Brian about her first visit to Winging It! and the amusing conversation she had there.			
4	Constance feels overdressed at the welcome dinner.			
5	Constance thinks Brian's friends acted ignorantly towards her.			
6	In 1968 Gina didn't open her business in Shaw because she was scared of riots after Martin Luther King's assassination.			
7	Constance doesn't care if anyone at Winging It! knows that she has a white boyfriend.			
8	The media coverage is different from what Constance has expected.			

5 Pair work

a) Use the internet to find out more about what is meant by the term "gentrification".

b) Exchange your findings with a partner. Talk about:

- the definition of "gentrification"
- causes of "gentrification"
- effects of "gentrification"
- different approaches to "gentrification": demographic-ecological, socio-cultural, political-economic, social movements, community networks
- gentrifier types

c) Explain why "gentrification" is an important issue in "Mambo Sauce".

d) Create a mind map to illustrate your findings.

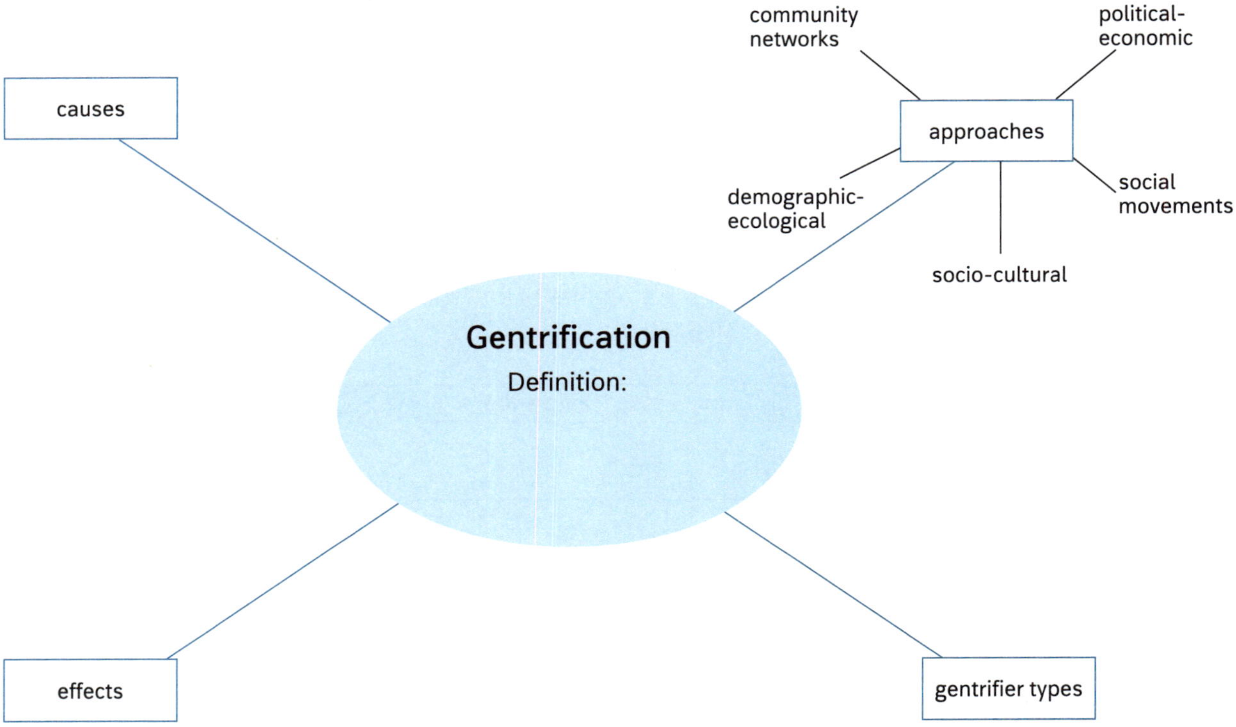

6

Evaluate the final sentence of the short story:
"This is what Brian didn't understand: once gentrification started it could not be stopped. And Constance was afraid love would do the same to her." (ll. 813–815)
What is meant by this? Do you agree with it?

POST-READING

7

Read the following quotes and fill in the grid. Note down the name of the character the quote refers to. In the last column, note down what the quote reveals about the character.

Quote		Character	What it reveals
1	"Brian wasn't who she had been looking for, in a place she didn't frequent." (ll. 3–4)		
2	"Connie, how many couples have you seen? The neighborhood is changing. I'm sure we won't be the only ones." (ll. 87–89)		
3	"Not every neighborhood needs to be Georgetown," [...]. (l. 346)		
4	"I wasn't a bitch. Don't you call me a bitch. You shared something you shouldn't have," [...]. (ll. 402–403)		
5	"They wanted to do something and they thought what the city needed was new black businesses, people who could show they believed in the city." (ll. 551–554)		
6	"It's been six months," [...]. (l. 721)		
7	"You think just because you black, you not changing this neighborhood?" [...]. (ll. 724–726)		
8	"No, I understand everything," [...]. (l. 789)		

8

The structure of a short story can often be divided into five parts. Identify the different parts in "Mambo Sauce" and explain their function. → **S11:** How to work with drama

rising action | exposition | resolution (denouement) | falling action | climax

Part	Lines	Function
1		
2		
3		
4		
5		

9
Analyse to what extent the conflict is resolved at the end of the story.

10
a) Explain why the author might have called her short story "Mambo Sauce".
b) Analyse the narrative perspective in "Mambo Sauce" and explain its purpose for the overall message of the story. → **Workshop:** Analysing narrative perspective
c) **Group work** Discuss other titles that you think would fit the story.

11
a) Read the definition of "ethnic identity" from the APA (American Psychological Association) Dictionary of Psychology.
b) Describe the aspects of Constance's ethnic identity depicted in the short story.

Info

Ethnic identity

An individual's sense of being a person who is defined, in part, by membership in a specific ethnic group. This sense is usually considered to be a complex construct involving shared social, cultural, linguistic, religious, and often racial factors but identical with none of them.

12
a) Explain what the narrator means by the following statement:
"Constance nodded, but she didn't want him coming into Winging It! with her. She didn't want them to know that she was with a white guy and that the way she talked when she was with them wasn't the way she talked when she was with him." (ll. 582–586)
b) Discuss possible consequences of the "them" and "us" mentality as shown in the extract above.
c) Analyse what issues of interracial relationships the couple is faced with in the short story. How could these challenges be met?

13
In class, discuss what the message of the short story "Mambo Sauce" is.

14
a) CHOOSE
Imagine Constance wants to explain her situation and her feelings to Brian. Write Constance's letter to Brian. → **S2:** Checklist: Creative writing
OR
Imagine Brian wants to explain to Constance how he feels about the incident at Winging it!. Write Brian's letter to Constance. → **S2:** Checklist: Creative writing
OR
Group work Discuss the following statement in your group:

"I believe in recognizing every human being as a human being – neither white, black, brown, or red; and when you are dealing with humanity as a family there's no question of integration or intermarriage. It's just one human being marrying another human being or one human being living around and with another human being."
– *Malcolm X, The Autobiography of Malcolm X*

b) Present your results in class.

Post-reading: The short stories

1 Group work

a) CHOOSE Get into groups of four to five students. Decide on a key scene of "Heads of the Colored People: Four Fancy Sketches, Two Chalk Outlines, and No Apology" **OR** "Mambo Sauce".

b) Create a freeze-frame. Your classmates can guess which scene you have chosen and explain why it is crucial for the overall message of the story.

2

Look at the following quotes taken from the two short stories that you have read. Choose the one you like best. Explain the context of the quote and analyse its relevance for the short story.

"We could see your work somewhere?" Gina asked.
"Probably in New York, one of those museums up there," Joy said.
"No, nowhere like that. Everything is just in the apartment right now," Constance said. At least this time she hadn't used "my apartment." "*The* apartment" betrayed no one.
– *"Mambo Sauce" (ll. 517–522)*

When he put his hand on Riley's shoulder, it was only because he disliked the sight of someone, especially one of his own, turning his back to him without hearing him out.
– *"Heads of the Colored People: Four Fancy Sketches, Two Chalk Outlines, and No Apology" (ll. 123–126)*

It had long irked Riley that his blackness or the degree of his loyalty to the cause should be suspect because he wore blue contacts and bleached his hair blond and because, on top of all that, his name was also Riley, and not, say, Tyreke.
– *"Heads of the Colored People: Four Fancy Sketches, Two Chalk Outlines, and No Apology" (ll. 98–102)*

"And what makes this place important?"
"It's a cornerstone of the community and when we allow developers to come in and take away these cornerstones, the whole structure collapses. [...]"
– *"Mambo Sauce" (ll. 668–671)*

I think a cop shooting is too melodramatic when the story was interesting on its own, and my preoccupation with race is perhaps overdone, [...].
– *"Heads of the Colored People: Four Fancy Sketches, Two Chalk Outlines, and No Apology" (ll. 412–414)*

"Mambo sauce," she said, wishing he hadn't brought it up.
"Oh yeah, we call it ghetto sauce," Alissa said. She laughed and the men joined. Constance strained a smile.
– *"Mambo Sauce" (ll. 313–316)*

3 Group work

Discuss what the quotes tell us about inequality in US society.

Ethnic identity and discrimination

1

a) Look at the cartoon and describe it.
b) Analyse the people shown in the cartoon.
c) Explain the message of the cartoon.

→ **Workshop:** Analysing a cartoon
→ **S17:** How to work with cartoons

Language support

The cartoon shows ...
On the left/right, you can see ...
The figure represents/symbolizes ...
The main issue addressed by the cartoon is ...
The message of the cartoon is ...

2

a) Do some research on the following terms:
- ethnic identity
- discrimination
- stereotype
- prejudice
- racism

b) Write your own definitions of these terms. How do they differ? → **S8:** How to improve your text
c) Find suitable examples from the short stories for each term and discuss them in class.

3 Pair work

a) **Think:** Each student deals with one of the two short stories.
Collect important aspects of
- ethnic identity
- discrimination
- racism

for each story. Use text references.
b) **Pair:** Compare your results with your partner showing differences and similarities.
c) Choose the short story you would recommend to someone interested in learning something about what it means to be African-American in the United States. Give reasons for your choice.
d) **Share** your results in class.

4 Pair work

Research some background information on police violence and the Black Lives Matter movement and present your findings in class.

5 Group work

Do some research on one of the following topics:

- the American Civil Rights Movement
- Martin Luther King Jr.
- the March on Washington
- Rosa Parks and the Montgomery Bus Boycott

Prepare a short presentation.

VIEWING: *WHAT IT MEANS TO BE BLACK AND GERMAN*

6

You are going to watch a video by DW News (Deutsche Welle) about Black Germans and their identity and achievements.

First read the questions below. Then watch the video and answer the questions. **Webcode** **DSW-73654-01**

a) What is the difference between the terms "Afro-German" and "Black German"?

____

____

b) What is "ISD" and how did it start?

____

____

c) Who was Audre Lorde?

____

____

d) What is the issue of "Black in Tech Berlin"?

____

____

e) How are Black studies, African history or colonial history taught in Germany?

____

____

f) Why are there so few Black German academics?

g) Who was "Milli" and why can she be considered as a gap in art history?

h) Which examples of Black Germans and their important works are given in the video?

i) What is "Each One Teach One"?

7 Group work

a) Watch the scene with Nana Titi Amoako (2:45–3:20) again. What does she say about white people? Explain what is meant by this statement.

b) Compare this statement with the depiction of Riley in "Heads of the Colored People: Four Fancy Sketches, Two Chalk Outlines, and No Apology".

8

Compare the reality of Black Germans as depicted in the video with the reality of African Americans as portrayed in the short stories. Discuss your results in class.

The Founder

PRE-VIEWING

1

You are going to watch the film *The Founder*, which was directed by John Lee Hancock (2016).

a) Look at the film poster and the film still below.

b) What do you think? What will the film be about? What kind of person may the protagonist Ray Kroc be? Make a mind map and note down your first ideas about the film.

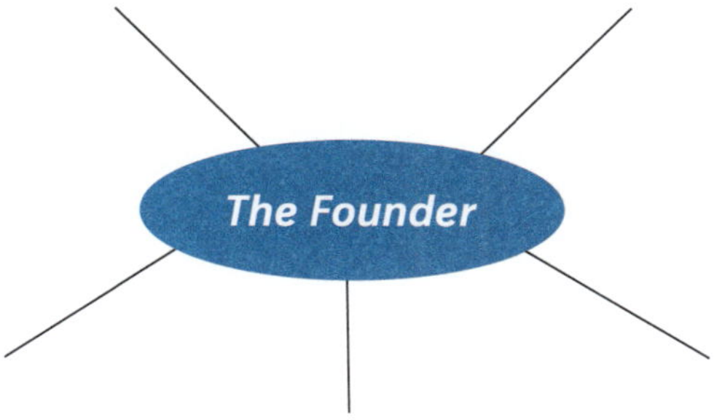

WHILE VIEWING

2

Look at the plot diagram and read the information below.
While you are watching the film, take notes and complete the plot diagram with the most important information.

Info

A **plot diagram** – key terms explained:

Exposition:	the introduction of the setting, the situation and the main characters
Rising action:	an important moment for the protagonist; the events focus on a conflict or a problem
Conflict:	a dramatic struggle between two forces; for example, character vs. character, character vs. society, or an inner conflict
Climax:	the point of highest tension; the turning point, which can change the protagonist's fate
Falling action:	the tension decreases and the main problem starts to resolve, leading to the ultimate resolution
Resolution:	the point when the conflict is finally (re)solved or determined unsolvable

The Founder **– Plot diagram:**

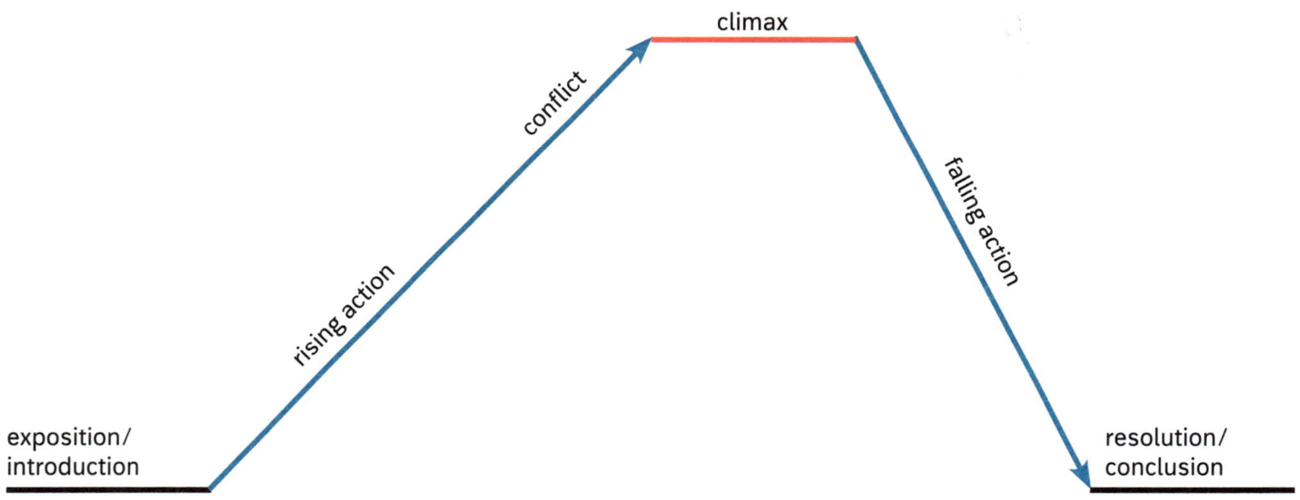

3

a) Sum up what the McDonald brothers tell Ray Kroc about their concept and the history of their business. (You can watch the following scenes again: 0:13:00 – 0:24:08)

b) Write a blog post on the McDonald brothers' idea. You can include your own experiences as a customer going to a restaurant.

→ **S7:** Checklist: Writing a blog post

4

Explain how Ray Kroc manages to make Dick and Mac McDonald's concept so successful.
You can create a chart to illustrate your findings.

5 **Pair work**

From the very first day, a pillar of McDonald's success has been quality management (QM). In the film Ray Kroc is shocked when he realizes that some of his franchisees and people who work in his restaurants do not stick to his quality standards.
What forms of quality management do you think are most important for McDonald's? Explain why.
The key words on the right can help you.

safety | supplies | food | products | cleanliness | financial | ...

6

a) Examine what skills and qualities Ray thinks people who want to work for McDonald's should have.

responsible | curious | fair | conscientious | stress-resistant | well-organized | highly motivated | reliable | resilient | sociable | cooperative | diligent | modest | independent | flexible | calm | determined | practical | creative | open-minded | ...

b) Write a job ad that Ray could have written. → **S8:** How to improve your text

7 → **S16:** Checklist: Analysis of a film scene → **Workshop:** Analysing a feature film

Watch the scene "Welcome to Minneapolis" (0:57:08 – 0:58:07) again.

Ray Kroc and Fred Turner have just landed in Minneapolis and a taxi has taken them to the opening of a new McDonald's franchise. The music starts, there is a close-up of Ray's shoe stepping out of the car, a tilting shot follows and the camera moves upwards – and Ray gets out of the car.

a) Describe your first impression of the scene.

b) Describe the two film stills and the cinematic effects used.

c) Analyse how Ray is presented in the scene and how the film-makers have accomplished this.

8 → **S16:** Checklist: Analysis of a film scene → **Workshop:** Analysing a feature film

a) Watch the scene in which Ray buys Dick and Mac out. Complete the viewing log below (you don't need to fill in every single box). You can look up cinematic devices on pp. 87–88 in your book.

time	setting/characters	what is going on/ what they are talking about	cinematic devices	function/effect
1:34:25 – 1:34:28	a dark conference room; Dick and Mac and their lawyer, Ray and his lawyer	the business partners and their lawyers are sitting at a table; Ray's lawyer explains that he agrees to the brothers' conditions of sale but with one exception	tracking shot from right to left, starting from behind the stairs; full shot of the conference table; the lighting is quite dark, shady	voyeuristic, it seems as if the viewer witnesses the scene from some distance
1:34:29 – 1:34:33		the 1% royalty for the brothers won't be written into the contract		
1:34:34 – 1:34:36		Mac is shocked and turns his head to his brother and back to Ray		
1:34:37 – 1:34:41			close-up of Ray	
1:34:41 – 1:34:44			close-up of Mac	
1:34:45 – 1:34:48			close-up of Ray	
1:34:49 – 1:34:57		Ray promises that the brothers will get their full royalties	quick shots showing close-ups of Dick, Mac and Ray	

time	setting/characters	what is going on/ what they are talking about	cinematic devices	function/effect
1:34:58 – 1:34:59			over the shoulder shot showing Dick, Mac and their lawyer	
1:35:00 – 1:35:02		Ray stands up and gives them his word	full shot of the conference table from below the stairs	
1:35:03 – 1:35:21			quick shots showing close-ups of Ray, Mac, including Ray's outstretched hand, and Dick; medium shot: Ray standing, the others sitting at the table	
1:35:22 – 1:35:25	Ray and his lawyer			
1:35:26 – 1:35:34			close-up of Mac	
1:35:34 – 1:35:49	Dick and Mac		medium shot, filmed through a glass pane; close-up of the cheques	

b) Analyse the scene focusing on the characters' emotions, the audience's possible reaction and how those are created through acting and cinematic devices.

9 → **S1:** Checklist: Summary

Write a plot summary of the film *The Founder*. You can use your plot diagram from p. 58.

POST-VIEWING

10 **Pair work**

a) At the beginning of the film, Ray is listening to the motivational record "The Power of the Positive" by Dr. Clarence Floyd Nelson (0:04:15 – 0:06:25). Read the extract from the film script below. Assess to what extent the scene foreshadows Ray's character traits and the way he acts to reach his goals.

> "Persistence. Nothing in the world can take the place of persistence.
> Talent won't. Nothing is more common than unsuccessful men with talent.
> Genius won't. Unrewarded genius is practically a cliché.
> Education won't. The world is full of educated fools.
> Persistence and determination alone are all powerful.
> Show that you don't have to be defeated by anything. That you can have peace of mind, improved health and a never ceasing flow of energy. If you attempt each and every day to achieve these things, the results will make themselves obvious to you. While it may sound like a magical notion, it is in you to create your own future. The greatest discovery of my generation is that human beings can alter their lives by altering their attitudes of mind.
> Or as Ralph Waldo Emerson declared, "A man is what he thinks about all day long.""

b) Compare this scene with the end of the film, when Ray is practising his speech in front of the mirror (1:39:25 – 1:40:20).

c) Comment on whether you agree or disagree with this attitude that persistence and determination are more important than talent or education in the world of work.

11 → **Workshop:** Analysing characters → **S8:** How to improve your text

Write a coherent text to characterize Ray.

12

Analyse the development of Ray's relationship with his wife Ethel.

13 → **Workshop:** Analysing characters → **S8:** How to improve your text

Choose one of the following characters and write a characterization.

- Fred Turner
- Harry Sonneborn
- Ethel Kroc
- Joan Kroc (previously Smith)
- Dick McDonald
- Mac McDonald

14

a) **Pair work** Choose two of the following quotes by Ray Kroc and explain in what contexts in the film they are said.

> "McDonald's can be the new American church. Feeding bodies and feeding souls and it ain't just open on Sundays, boys. It's open seven days a week." (0:34:04 – 0:34:18)

> "Contracts are like hearts, they're made to be broken." (1:25:53 – 1:25:57)

> "Business is war. It's dog eat dog, rat eat rat. If my competitor were drowning, I'd walk over and I'd put a hose right in his mouth." (1:29:24 – 1:29:33)

> "Now, I know what you're thinking. How the heck does a 52-year-old, over the hill, milkshake machine salesman, build a fast food empire with 1600 restaurants, in 50 states, five foreign countries, with an annual revenue of in the neighborhood of 700 million dollars? One word, persistence." (1:39:25 – 1:39:52)

b) **Group work** Comment on the quotes: which ones do you agree or disagree with? Give reasons for your answers.

15 Group work

Discuss whether Ray Kroc can be considered an exceptional founder. Comment on the film title, too.

16

Film directors and screenwriters often adapt real facts for a more dramatic effect, which is called 'artistic licence'. What is fiction and what is reality? What may be exaggerated, what was left out, what did not really happen? Check some facts and research how accurate the film is if you compare it with the historic events.

Ray Kroc, Chairman of the Board of the McDonald's Corporation

Fiction?	Reality?

17

a) Write a film review on *The Founder*.

Info

Tips on how to write a film review:

- Come up with a catchy heading for your review.
- Name essential information about the film (title, release date, genre, director, screenwriter, producer).
- Give a short plot summary, but do not give away too much of the story (such as a twist or the end) as you might spoil the film for a possible audience.
- Describe your personal impression of the film.
- Comment on the actors. (Were they convincing? Were they a good choice for the roles?)
- Describe how the cinematic devices contribute to the effect of the film (e.g. camera, editing, lighting, sound, special effects, ...).
- Finally, say whether you would recommend the film (and, if so, to whom/what kind of audience). Give the film a rating (1–10 stars) and explain your decision.

b) Use the internet to find out how other viewers have rated the film. Think about whether you would like to upload your film review, too.

The American Dream

1

Read the information below.

Info

The American Dream

The American Dream is a concept that generations of people in the United States have believed in and strived for. The term was coined by James Truslow Adams in his book *The Epic of America* (1931):

"The American Dream is that dream of a land in which life should be better and richer and fuller for everyone, with opportunity for each according to ability or achievement."

The American Dream is rooted in the Declaration of Independence (July 4, 1776), a document signed by the Thirteen Colonies seeking independence from British rule:

"We hold these truths to be self-evident, that all men are created equal, that they are endowed by their Creator with certain unalienable Rights, that among these are Life, Liberty and the pursuit of Happiness."

– Preamble to the Declaration of Independence

For many people, the American Dream means that everybody has the freedom to do what they want and everybody who works hard can be successful and rise "from rags to riches".

2 Group work

There is a variety of individual interpretations of the American Dream, for example:

- getting rich, making it
- climbing up the social ladder
- leading a happy life
- living peacefully
- having a happy family and home
- being independent
- knowing that everything is possible
- doing what you love
- being able to do good in the world
- being self-employed
- owning your own company
- practising your religion freely
- being able to say your opinion
- being treated equally, no matter who you are or where you are from
- ...

What do you think about the American Dream and the different interpretations? Can the American Dream come true for everybody? Discuss in your group.

3 Pair work

What is the American Dream for the following characters from the film *The Founder*? What is similar and what is different? Note down some ideas and fill in the Venn diagram below.

The American Dream for characters in *The Founder*

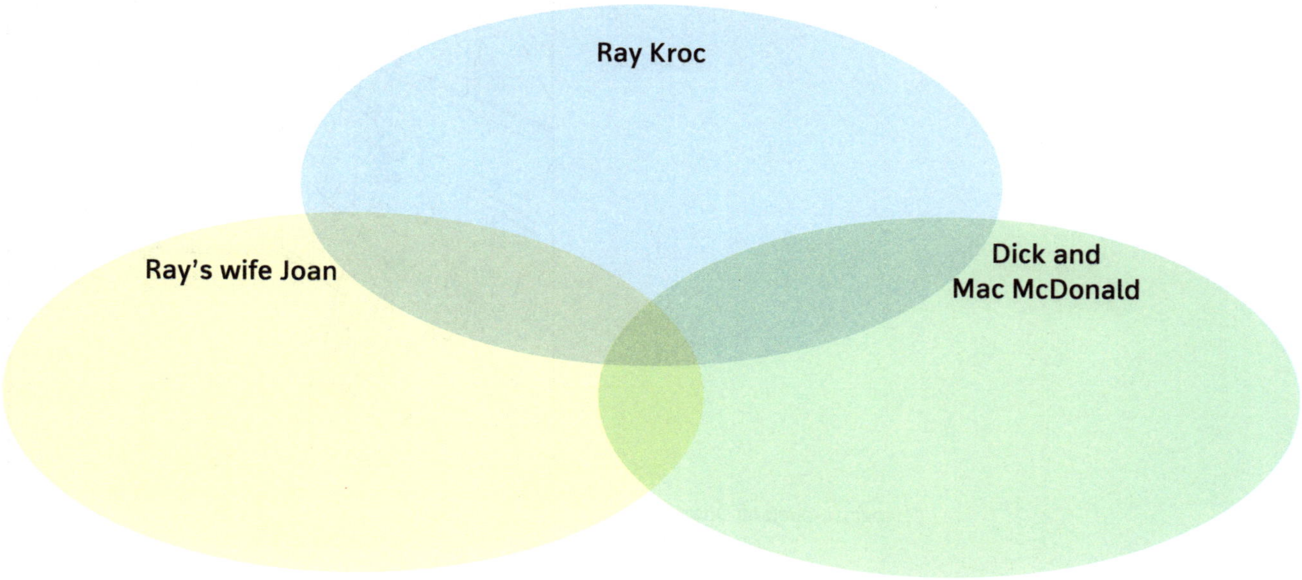

4 Pair work

You are going to watch the CNBC video "Why McDonald's Failed In Iceland".

a) Pre-viewing: As the title of the documentary suggests, McDonald's tried to establish their business in Iceland. Despite being successful in more than 100 countries around the world, they failed in Iceland. Name possible reasons. Share your ideas with a partner.

b) Now watch the video. **Webcode** DSW-73654-02
While you are watching, list the reasons for McDonald's failure in Iceland. Compare your assumptions from a) with the actual reasons. Which aspects were you right about and which aspects were you wrong about?

c) Post-viewing: Imagine McDonald's wants to return to Iceland and make another attempt to establish their franchise there. Fill in the grid below. Then write a short text giving some advice to the McDonald's management.

McDonald's in Iceland?	
Things they can count on	**Hurdles to overcome**

Ethics in the world of business

1

Research online how McDonald's presents itself as a company. Find out more about their beliefs and values, priorities and activities. Present your findings in class.

2 → **Workshop:** Analysing a cartoon → **S17:** How to work with cartoons

Look at the cartoon and describe it. Explain the message of the cartoon.

"Hangin' around McDonald's again, aren't you?"

3 → **S15:** How to describe pictures

McDonald's has been criticised for different reasons. Look at the photos below and describe the different forms of protest against McDonald's.

4

Use the internet to find out more about the different reasons why McDonald's has been criticised. Present your findings in class.

5 **Pair work**

Examine how both positive and negative aspects of McDonald's are presented in the film *The Founder*.

6 **Group work**

Discuss whether or not you would like to work for McDonald's. Give reasons for your answers.

7 → **S3:** Checklist: Formal letter

Choose an international company that you find interesting. Use the internet to find out more about the company, their beliefs and values, and possible careers. Write a letter of application to the company.

MEDIATION

8 → **Workshop:** Mediation → **S19:** How to improve your mediation skills → **S5:** Checklist: Writing a speech

You are taking part in an international youth conference on environmental protection and sustainability. Read the article from the online magazine *BASIC thinking*. Use the information to prepare a speech for the conference. Explain how McDonald's has been working on changing its image in Germany and how the company can still improve.

Wie nachhaltig ist McDonald's Deutschland wirklich?

30. Mrz 2021
geschrieben von Marinela Potor

Im Klimacheck von *BASIC thinking* stellen wir die Nachhaltigkeitsstrategien von Konzernen auf den Prüfstand. Wie nachhaltig und grün sind die neuen Konzepte wirklich? Diesmal: McDonald's Deutschland.

Es war ein großes Zeichen, als McDonald's im Februar 2021 eine dreijährige Partnerschaft mit Beyond Meat ankündigte. Das Unternehmen für vegane Produkte soll für McDonald's weltweit den pflanzlichen McPlant-Burger liefern.
Solche Kooperationen sind fürs Klima weitreichender als man denkt. Sie signalisieren schließlich Produzenten und Lieferanten weltweit, dass der Trend weg vom Fleisch und hin zu pflanzenbasierter Ernährung geht.
Und auch McDonald's positioniert sich damit als Unternehmen, das verstärkt auf Klimaschutz achten will. Doch wie sieht das über den veganen Burger hinaus aus? Wir schauen uns die aktuelle Nachhaltigkeitsstrategie der Fast-Food-Kette in Deutschland an. [...]

Regionale Priorität
Tatsächlich hat sich McDonald's Deutschland hier sehr bewusst für eine möglichst regionale Versorgung entschieden. Bis auf Tomaten, Zwiebeln, Kaffee sowie Shrimps und Fisch, die aus Europa oder aus weltweiten Quellen stammen, kommt die Mehrheit der Produkte aus Deutschland.
Das reduziert natürlich Lieferwege. Als Qualitätssiegel setzt McDonald's auf Nachhaltigkeitszertifikate.

Bio-Siegel und Co.
Dazu gehört das Bio-Siegel bei Obst und Gemüse. Das ist natürlich nicht das strikteste aller Nachhaltigkeitssiegel, aber immerhin.
Fischprodukte stammen zu 100 Prozent per MSC-Label und ASC-Label aus nachhaltiger Fischerei und der Kaffee kommt von Farmen, die zur Rainforest-Alliance gehören.

Tierhaltung
Bei den Hühnern achtet das Unternehmen darauf, dass die Tiere mit gentechnisch unveränderten vegetarischen Futtermitteln gefüttert werden und der Einsatz von Antibiotika gemindert wird. Heißt aber auch: Die Hähnchenprodukte sind nicht durchweg frei von Antibiotika.
Zur Tierhaltung der Hühner sagte McDonald's gegenüber *BASIC thinking*, dass alle Hühnerprodukte zu 100 Prozent von Tieren aus Freilandhaltung kämen.
Für Rindfleisch gibt es seit 2019 das Programm „Best Beef". Damit fördert das Unternehmen Rindbauern, die in ihren Nachhaltigkeitsansätzen über das gesetzlich erforderliche Minimum hinausgehen. Das Schweinefleisch kommt sowohl von männlichen (nicht-kastrierten) und weiblichen Tieren und stammt aus dem Qualitätsprogramm QS. Dazu gehören sowohl artgerechte Fütterung als auch Transport.
Wie bereits erwähnt ist auch die neue Partnerschaft mit Beyond Meat und dem Ausrollen von veganen Burgern ein weiterer Aspekt für mehr Klimaschutz. Ebenfalls positiv: Den Januar 2021 erklärte McDonald's zum „Veganuary."

Verpackung
Als Fast-Food-Kette sind Verpackungen für McDonald's natürlich ein großes Thema. Hier hat das Unternehmen aber bereits einen grünen Ansatz.
Dessertverpackungen (Strohhalme, Eisbecher, Löffel) sind schon komplett plastikfrei. Für Einwegbecher (aus Papier) gibt es ein Recyclingprogramm, um daraus bedruckbare Papierbögen zu machen.
Die Happy-Meal-Verpackungen sind noch nicht komplett plastikfrei. Doch man bemüht sich, zunehmend mehr Papier und weniger Plastik zu nutzen. Das Spielzeug ist aber weiterhin aus Plastik. [...]

Einweg-Papier ist auch Verschwendung
Klar ist: Diese Strategie stammt vor der neuen Vorgabe der Bundesregierung, die Einweg-Plastik verbietet. Tatsächlich hat McDonald's sein Plastikproblem aber schon so gut wie gelöst. Nur: Auch

Einweg-Papier ist im Grunde Ressourcenvergeudung.
Bis 2025 soll es aber nur noch Verpackungen aus erneuerbarem, recyceltem oder zertifiziertem Material geben. [...]

Energie

Im Bereich „Energie" konzentriert sich die Nachhaltigkeitsstrategie des Konzerns in Deutschland vor allem auf zwei Säulen: Mobilität und Strom.

Ökostrom und E-Autos

So nutzen die Betriebe in Deutschland zu 100 Prozent Strom aus Wasserkraft. [...]
Beim eigenen Fuhrpark setzt sich der Konzern Grenzwerte und bemüht sich zumindest die E-Flotte auszubauen. [...]
So bietet das Unternehmen seinen Mitarbeitern auch ein günstiges Fahrradleasing an (auch mit E-Bikes). Auch bei den Lieferungen setzt McDonald's in Deutschland offenbar auf zwei Räder. [...]

Fazit zur Nachhaltigkeitsstrategie von McDonald's in Deutschland

Verglichen mit den Anfängen von McDonald's hat die Fast-Food-Kette einen großen Wandel vollzogen. Klar: Schnelles Essen ist immer noch das Konzept und allein das mögen viele aus Klimasicht kritisieren.
Dennoch bemüht sich die Restaurantkette eindeutig um einen niedrigeren CO_2-Fußabdruck. In vielen Bereichen, wie etwa beim Recycling, Ökostrom oder der regionalen Produkt- und Lieferkette ist schon ein großes Bewusstsein für den Klimaschutz zu erkennen, auch wenn sicherlich noch Luft nach oben besteht.
Lobenswert ist auch der Transparenz-Ansatz des Unternehmens. Wer will, findet online oder per App eine detaillierte Auflistung aller Zutaten in den einzelnen Produkten. [...]

Wasserstrategie fehlt

Auffällig ist aber, dass McDonald's bestimmte Bereiche in seiner Nachhaltigkeitsstrategie gar nicht erst erwähnt.
Dazu gehören zum Beispiel:
- die Zubereitung der Gerichte
- Zusatzstoffe in Gerichten
- Wasserkonsum

Wie viel Wasser verbraucht McDonald's Deutschland beispielsweise in der gesamten Produktkette? Gibt es Ansätze, um Wasser zu sparen oder auch wenn möglich zu recyceln?
Auf Nachfrage von *BASIC thinking* sagt das Unternehmen, dass verantwortungsbewusstes Wassermanagement durchaus Teil der Nachhaltigkeitsstrategie sei.
„In Deutschland folgen wir diesem Grundsatz. So wurden unsere Restaurants unter anderem mit entsprechenden Reinigungsanlagen ausgestattet, um eine Abwasserbelastung möglichst zu minimieren", sagt das Unternehmen gegenüber *BASIC thinking*.

Was ist mit Plastikflaschen?

Und: Was ist eigentlich mit den Wasser- und Getränkeprodukten in den Restaurants? Diese werden nach wie vor in Plastik verpackt. Auch hier könnte sich die Kette künftig nachhaltigere Alternativen überlegen, die es ja durchaus gibt.
Dazu sagt McDonald's Deutschland Folgendes: „Apfelschorle und Wasser werden derzeit in Einwegpfandgebinden angeboten, da diese aus Verpackungs- und Recyclingprozessgesichtspunkten so bestmöglich in einen optimierten und geschlossenen Kreislauf zurückgeführt werden können."
Angesichts eines sehr guten Mehrwegsystems von Glasflaschen in Deutschland, ist dies aber nicht zu 100 Prozent nachvollziehbar.

Soziale Verantwortung von Fast Food

Die Zutaten der Gerichte wie Transfette, Zucker oder auch Stärken mögen etwa im Vergleich zu Fleisch keinen extremen Klimaeffekt haben. Doch sie schaden den Konsumentinnen und Konsumenten.
Menschen, die sehr viel Fast Food konsumieren, leiden öfter an Depressionen, ihre Haut altert schneller und Fast Food begünstigt auch Krankheiten wie Diabetes Typ 2 und Demenz.
Fairerweise muss man dazu sagen, dass dies meist daran liegt, dass Menschen, die viel Fast Food essen auch wenig Sport treiben und anderweitig ungesund unterwegs sind. Auch wird mal ein Burger hier oder dort keine Langzeitschäden hervorrufen.
Dennoch gäbe es in diesen Bereichen durchaus noch Verbesserungspotenzial für McDonald's. Darin steckt aber auch eine wirtschaftliche Herausforderung. Denn als günstige Fast-Food-Kette hat McDonald's natürlich auch einen strikten Price-Point.

Wer will schon so viel für einen Burger bei „Mickie D's“ zahlen wie in einem Gourmet-Restaurant?

McDonald's muss mit der Zeit gehen

Gleichzeitig sieht natürlich auch der Konzern, dass sich das Bewusstsein der Kundinnen und Kunden wandelt, hin zu mehr Nachhaltigkeit und einem gesünderen Lifestyle. Fettige Pommes sind da einfach nicht mehr zeitgemäß.

Es wird daher spannend zu sehen, wie McDonald's künftig mit den Verbraucherinnen und Verbrauchern mitgehen wird und gleichzeitig wirtschaftlich bleiben kann.

Notes for your speech:

Religion and sexual diversity

1 → **S15:** How to describe pictures

a) Look at the two photos below and describe them.

b) Pair work Talk to your neighbour:
- Explain in what way the two pictures deal with the same topic.
- Compare the pictures.
- Assess why the two pictures are contradictory.

GETTING STARTED – SEXUAL DIVERSITY

2 Think – Pair – Share

What do you know about queer people?

3

What do you think? Read five statements from *DoSomething.org* on queer youth life in America. Match the given percentages to the statements below.

90% | 42% | 80% | 92% | 60%

1. __________ of people who are LGBT report living in an unwelcoming environment.
2. __________ of gay and lesbian youth report severe social isolation.
3. __________ of LGBT students report feeling unsafe at school because of their sexual orientation. [...]
4. __________ of teens who are LGBT come out to their close friends.
5. In 2013, __________ of adults who are LGBT said they believe society had become more accepting of them than in the past 10 years. [...]

LOVE IS LOVE – TERMS AND CONCEPTS REGARDING SEXUAL DIVERSITY

4

Love is love and it comes in many forms and facets. For a long time, there was talk of LGBTQ+. This acronym has now been extended as follows: LGBTQQIP2SAA. It stands for lesbian, gay, bisexual, transgender, queer, questioning, intersex, pansexual, two-spirit (2S), androgynous and asexual. Moreover, people define themselves as cisgender or non-binary. Match each term with its suitable description.

Term		Description	
1	lesbian	A	... describes the lack of a sexual attraction or desire for other people.
2	gay	B	... describes people who naturally (without any medical interventions) develop primary and/or secondary sex characteristics that do not fit neatly into society's definitions of male or female.
3	bisexual	C	... describes a woman who is emotionally, romantically, or sexually attracted to other women.
4	transgender	D	... describes a person who is not limited in sexual choice with regard to biological sex, gender, or gender identity.
5	queer	E	... describes a person who is emotionally, romantically, or sexually attracted to members of the same gender.
6	questioning	F	... describes a third gender in a ceremonial or social role found in some Native American cultures, often involving birth-assigned men or women taking on the identities and roles of the opposite sex; a sacred and historical identity, which can include but is by no means limited to LGBTQ identities.
7	intersex	G	... describes a person who is emotionally, romantically, or sexually attracted to more than one sex, gender or gender identity though not necessarily simultaneously, in the same way or to the same degree.
8	pansexual	H	... describes people who are in the process of exploring their sexual orientation or gender identity.
9	two-spirit (2S)	I	... refers to people identifying and/or presenting as neither distinguishably masculine nor feminine.
10	androgynous	J	... is seen as an umbrella term for people whose gender identity and/or expression is different from cultural expectations based on the sex they were assigned at birth. However, it does not imply any specific sexual orientation. These people may identify as straight, gay, lesbian, bisexual, etc.
11	asexual	K	... is used as an umbrella term for people who are not straight or cisgender. People often use it to express fluid identities and orientations.
12	cisgender	L	... describes a person whose gender identity corresponds with the sex assigned to them at birth.
13	non-binary	M	... describes a person who does not identify exclusively as a man or a woman. They may identify as being both a man and a woman, somewhere in between, or as falling completely outside these categories.

1	2	3	4	5	6	7	8	9	10	11	12	13

THE BIBLE BELT

5

Look at the map and read the information below.

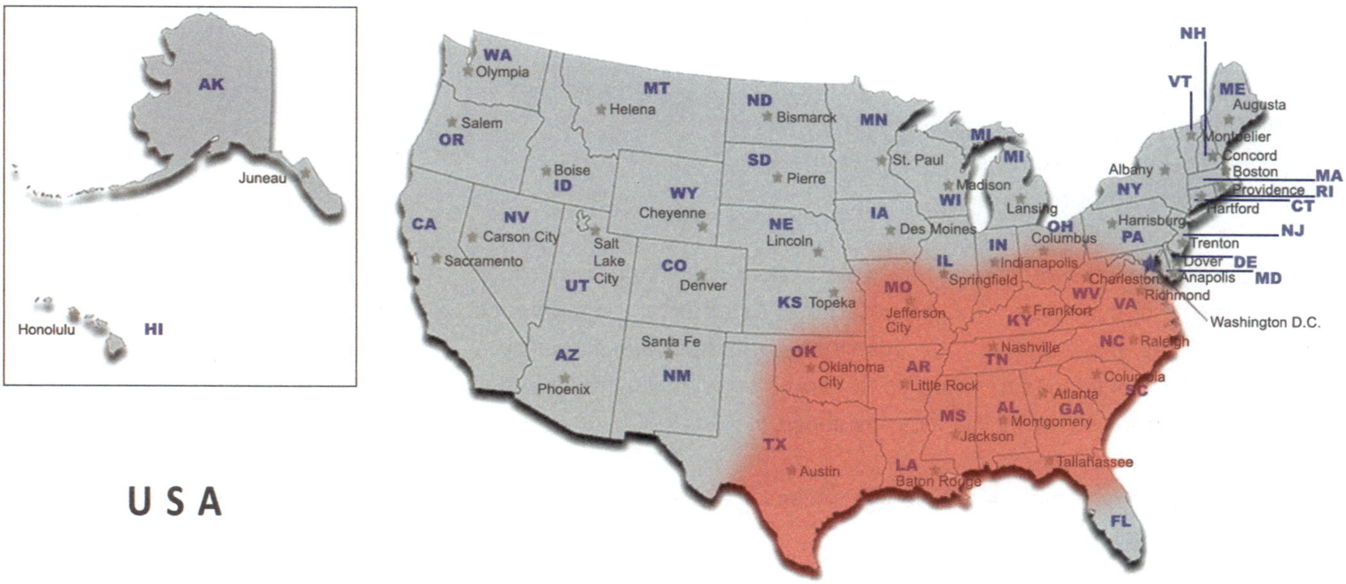

Info

The Bible Belt

The "Bible Belt" includes several southern states in the United States and runs like a kind of belt from Texas to the southeast. The southern states are typically the stronghold of the Bible Belt due to the colonial foundations of state religions in the area. It is a region of highly conservative, religiously determined people whose beliefs in part stem from the Christian Bible.
One of the Bible Belt states is Arkansas. It got the official nickname "The Natural State" in 1995. Before that, it was called "Land of Opportunity" for about 40 years.

6 → **Workshop:** Analysing a cartoon → **S17:** How to work with cartoons

a) Look at the cartoon and describe it.
b) Examine the message of the cartoon.
c) **Think – Pair – Share** Think about what gay life might look like in Arkansas and state your speculations.

Language support

- When I first saw the cartoon, I thought / felt / was reminded of ...
- My initial thought when seeing the cartoon was ...
- The cartoon illustrates / shows / depicts / deals with / points out ...
- It shows / deals with / refers to / comments on ...
- In the cartoon there is/are ... / there seems to be ... / one can see ...
- In the foreground/background ...
- In the middle/centre ...
- At the top/bottom ...
- On the right/left ...
- In the top left-hand corner ... / In the bottom right-hand corner ...
- The cartoon implies ... / is supposed to ... / stands for ... / represents ... / is a caricature of ...
- It can be assumed that ... because it brings its message across by ...
- The cartoonist tries to / aims to / intends to / is making fun of / criticizes / draws attention to ...
- The cartoonist skillfully/effectively shows ...
- In my opinion, ...
- I believe/think that the cartoon is convincing / too abstract / well composed / authentic / simplistic / confusing / ... because ...

7

a) Look at the symbols of different religions and spiritual/faith communities below. Do you know all of them? Which ones are unknown to you?

b) **Group work** Do some research on the following question:
Do the religions/faith communities officially accept/tolerate other sexual orientations or gender identities next to being heterosexual and cisgender? If not, what is their standpoint?
Present your results in a poster.

8

While the picture above represents Christianity as one religion, it can have different forms and facets just like all the other religions and faith communities, too. Baptism is one of those forms. Do some research on the Southern Baptist Convention, which is the largest religious group in Arkansas, USA.

a) Outline the religious community in general.

b) State information regarding their viewpoint on homosexuality and diverse gender orientations.

CONVERSION THERAPY

9

Read the information below.

Info

Conversion therapy

Conversion therapy (sometimes also known as Sexual Orientation and Gender Identity Change Efforts) refers to a wide range of different interventions that aim to change or suppress a person's sexual orientation, sexual expression or gender identity. Diverse practices and measures are used with the aim to change people from homosexual or bisexual to heterosexual and from trans or gender diverse to cisgender.
Next to private or public mental health care centres, religious or faith-based organizations have designed programmes of conversion therapy that see forms of sexuality other than being heterosexual and cisgender as a sin and so must be changed. The conversion practices are often represented as part of spiritual healing, mental health and religious freedom.
Believing that LGBTQ people are inferior and weak, the practices of conversion therapy are degrading and discriminatory. They often result in long-lasting psychological and physical damage. Although conversion practices are often represented in the media as outdated and homophobic, some countries and regions still allow conversion therapy on a legal basis.

10 → **Workshop:** Analysing a cartoon → **S17:** How to work with cartoons

a) Look at the cartoon and describe it.
b) Explain what the customer in the cartoon might have misunderstood.
c) Analyse in what way the cartoonist criticizes conversion therapy with his/her mode of presentation.

11

You are going to listen to John Smid, a former gay conversion therapist who is talking about conversion therapy in an interview with *60 Minutes Australia*. Watch the video and answer the following questions.

Webcode DSW-73654-03

a) What does the Bible say about homosexuality?

____

____

b) Why do people interpret the Bible with an anti-gay bias according to John Smid?

____

____

c) Which practices are common in gay conversion therapy?

____

____

d) According to John Smid, these practices did not work. Which consequences did the people instead suffer from after gay conversion therapy?

e) How does John Smid feel now about himself having been a conversion therapist?

12

Do some more research on conversion therapy and give answers to the following questions.

a) Which other practices and therapy measures are known of?
b) In which countries and/or regions is conversion therapy still legal?
c) Which countries officially banned conversion therapy and why?

13

Use the information from the info box (p. 75), the interview Webcode DSW-73654-03 and your own research to create an infographic about conversion therapy that includes all the important information.

Info

Infographics

An infographic is a concise visualization of a subject's most important facts on one single page using headings, bullet points and/or images and tables. Effective infographics split the information into different sections. The following guidelines will help you.

✓ 1. Organize your research well.
✓ 2. Make a simple outline.
✓ 3. Think of informative header information.
✓ 4. Design or choose an infographic template.
✓ 5. State your facts concisely.
✓ 6. Publish and present your fact file.

Tip: You may use free software tools to create your infographic.

Discrimination

Pre-viewing: Do not erase who you are

Every day people of different ethnic or social groups experience discrimination in various forms and facets. Being discriminated against because of who you are is also a major theme in the film *Boy Erased* (2018). In order to understand the underlying mechanisms, familiarize yourself with stereotypes and related concepts as well as with the different forms of discrimination.

STEREOTYPES – THE BASIS OF DISCRIMINATION

1

Read the information below.

Info

- A **stereotype** is a judgement (in the sense of an opinion) that can be adopted about specific types of individuals or certain ways of doing things. These thoughts or beliefs may or may not reflect reality accurately. It can be differentiated into:
  - an **autostereotype**, which is a judgement (in the sense of an opinion) that one group forms about itself. The autostereotype is often more differentiated than the heterostereotype. The positive attributes are dominating.
  - a **heterostereotype**, which is used by a group to define others. The heterostereotype tends to be a black-or-white pattern: it can be a stronger generalization or simplification.
- A **prejudice** is an unfair and unreasonable opinion or feeling of dislike of a person or group, especially when it is formed without enough thought or knowledge.
- A **cliché** is a popular or common idea or phrase that has lost originality and ingenuity by long overuse.

2

a) Using your knowledge from the info box above, decide whether the following statements are a stereotype (autostereotype or heterostereotype), a prejudice or a cliché. Draw lines.

autostereotype	Some foreigners believe that "all Germans are Nazis or fascists."
heterostereotype	A queer woman states: "Homosexuals are good lovers."
prejudice	A German friend of mine states: "All Latinos dance well."
cliché	"All gay men are hairdressers."

b) Pair work Talk to your neighbour:
- Have you ever been confronted with stereotypes and/or prejudices?
- If so, how did you feel? What did you do?
- If not, can you imagine how people might feel when being valued solely on the basis of stereotypes and prejudices?

FORMS OF DISCRIMINATION

3

Read the article "Discrimination" by Amnesty International. In order to raise awareness for discriminatory practices in everyday life, prepare an infographic (cf. the info box on p. 76) in which you define discrimination, describe possible forms of discrimination, and state the consequences of discrimination.

Discrimination

OVERVIEW

Discrimination strikes at the very heart of being human. It is harming someone's rights simply because of who they are or what they believe. Discrimination is harmful and perpetuates[1] inequality.

We all have the right to be treated equally, regardless of our race, ethnicity, nationality, class, [...] religion, belief, sex, gender, language, sexual orientation, gender identity, sex characteristics, age, health or other status. Yet all too often we hear heartbreaking stories of people who suffer cruelty simply for belonging to a "different" group from those in positions of privilege or power.

Discrimination occurs when a person is unable to enjoy his or her human rights or other legal rights on an equal basis with others because of an unjustified distinction made in policy, law or treatment. [...]

Discrimination can take various forms:

Direct discrimination is when an explicit distinction is made between groups of people that results in individuals from some groups being less able than others to exercise their rights. For example, a law that requires women, and not men, to provide proof of a certain level of education as a prerequisite for voting would constitute direct discrimination on the grounds of sex.

Indirect discrimination is when a law, policy, or practice is presented in neutral terms (that is, no explicit distinctions are made) but it disproportionately disadvantages a specific group or groups. For example, a law that requires everyone to provide proof of a certain level of education as a prerequisite for voting has an indirectly discriminatory effect on any group that is less likely to have achieved that level of education (such as disadvantaged ethnic groups or women).

Intersectional discrimination is when several forms of discrimination combine to leave a particular group or groups at an even greater disadvantage. For example, discrimination against women frequently means that they are paid less than men for the same work. Discrimination against an ethnic minority often results in members of that group being paid less than others for the same work. Where women from a minority group are paid less than other women and less than men from the same minority group, they are suffering from intersectional discrimination on the grounds of their sex, gender and ethnicity. [...]

WHAT DRIVES DISCRIMINATION?

At the heart of all forms of discrimination is prejudice based on concepts of identity, and the need to identify with a certain group. This can lead to division, hatred and even the dehumanization of other people because they have a different identity.

In many parts of the world, the politics of blame and fear is on the rise. Intolerance, hatred and discrimination is causing an ever-widening rift in societies. [...]

SOME KEY FORMS OF DISCRIMINATION

Racial and ethnic discrimination

Racism affects virtually every country in the world. It systematically denies people their full human rights just because of their colour, race, ethnicity, descent[2] [...] or national origin. Racism unchecked can fuel large-scale atrocities[3] such as the 1994 genocide in Rwanda and more recently, apartheid and ethnic cleansing of the Rohingya people in Myanmar. [...]

Discrimination against non-nationals, sometimes known as xenophobia

[...] discrimination against non-nationals is frequently based on racism or notions of superiority [...].

Since 2008, South Africa has experienced several outbreaks of violence against refugees, asylum seekers and migrants from other African countries, including killings, and looting or burning of shops and businesses. In some instances, the violence has been inflamed by the hate-filled rhetoric of politicians who have wrongly labelled foreign nationals "criminals" and accused them of burdening the health system.

Annotations

[1] to **perpetuate** = to make something such as a bad situation, belief, etc. continue for a long time

[2] **descent** = a person's family origins

[3] **atrocity** = a cruel and violent act, especially in a war

Discrimination has also been a feature of the response of authorities to refugees and asylum seekers in other parts of the world. Many people in countries receiving refugees and asylum-seekers view the situation as a crisis with leaders and politicians exploiting these fears by promising, and in some cases enacting, abusive and unlawful policies.

For example, Hungary passed a package of punitive laws in 2018, which target groups that the government has identified as supporting refugees and migrants. The authorities have also subjected refugees and asylum seekers to violent push-backs and ill-treatment and imposed arbitrary detention on those attempting to enter Hungarian territory. [...]

Discrimination against lesbian, gay, bisexual, transgender and intersex (LGBTI) people

Everywhere in the world, people face discrimination because of who they love, who they are attracted to and who they are. Lesbian, gay, bisexual, transgender and intersex (LGBTI) people risk being unfairly treated in all areas of their lives, whether it's in education, employment, housing or access to health care, and they may face harassment and violence.

Some countries punish people for their sexual orientation or their gender identity with jail or even death. For example, in October 2019, Uganda's Ethics and Integrity Minister announced that the government was planning to introduce the death penalty for consensual same-sex sexual acts. [...]

It is extremely difficult, and in most cases, impossible for LGBTI people to live their lives freely and seek justice for abuses when the laws are not on their side. Even when they are, there is strong stigma and stereotyping of LGBTI identities that prevents them from living their lives as equal members of society or accessing rights and freedoms that are available to others. That's why LGBTI activists campaign relentlessly for their rights: whether it's to be free from discrimination to love who they want, have their gender legally recognized or to just be protected from the risk of assault and harassment. [...]

Gender discrimination

In many countries, in all regions of the world, laws, policies, customs and beliefs exist that deny women and girls their rights.

By law, women cannot dress as they like (Saudi Arabia, Iran) or work at night (Madagascar) or take out a loan without their husband's signature (Equatorial Guinea). In many countries, discriminatory laws place limits on a woman's right to divorce, own property, exercise control over her own body and enjoy protection from harassment.

In the ongoing battle for justice, hundreds of thousands of women and girls take to the streets to claim their human rights and demand gender equality. In the USA, Europe and Japan, women protested against misogyny[4] and abuse as part of the #MeToo marches. In Argentina, Ireland and Poland, women demonstrated to demand a stop to oppressive abortion laws. In Saudi Arabia, they called for an end to the driving ban, and in Iran, they demanded an end to forced *hijab* (veiling[5]).

All over the world, women and girls have been at the forefront of demands for change.

Yet despite the stratospheric rise of women's activism, the stark reality remains that many governments around the world openly support policies, laws and customs that subjugate[6] and suppress women. [...]

Discrimination based on disability

As many as 1 in 10 people around the world lives with a disability. Yet in many societies, people with disabilities must grapple with stigma, being ostracized[7] and treated as objects of pity or fear.

Developing countries are home to about 80 per cent of people with disabilities. The overwhelming majority of people with disabilities – 82 per cent – live below the poverty line. Women with disabilities are two to three times more likely to encounter physical and sexual abuse than women without disabilities.

In Kazakhstan, current laws mean that thousands of people with psychosocial and intellectual disabilities have been declared "incapable" by law and put in the care of a guardian. Under this system they cannot exercise their rights and are not able to challenge the decision in court. [...]

Annotations

[4] **misogyny** = a feeling of hate or dislike towards women, or a feeling that women are not as good as men

[5] **veil** = a piece of thin soft cloth worn by women to cover their head or face

[6] to **subjugate** = to take complete control of somebody

[7] **ostracized** = excluded

DIVERSITY AND DISCRIMINATION

4 CHALLENGE

Look at the graphic "Diversity Wheel" below.

a) Describe which categories are used to describe a personality.

b) Examine which of these categories are naturally given and which are socially constructed. Give reasons.

c) Discuss whether it is legitimate to put people in categories that are not natural but socially constructed and to discriminate against them on that basis.

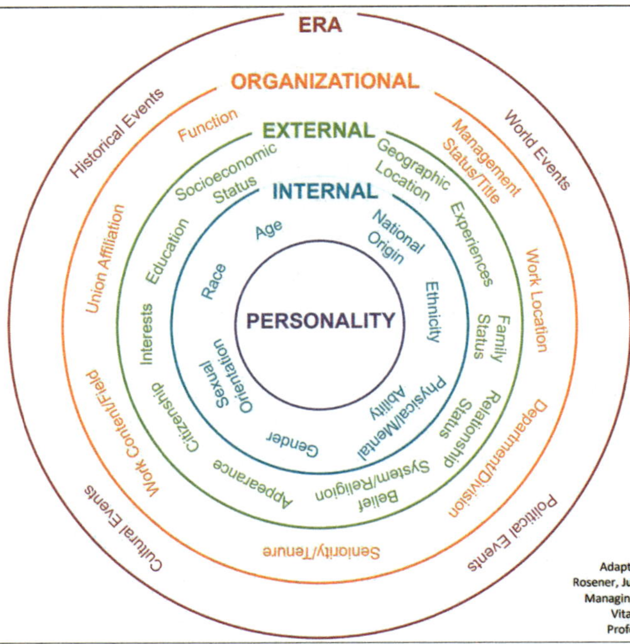

Adapted from: Loden, Marily & Rosener, Judy, "Workforce America! Managing Employee Diversity as a Vital Resource," McGraw-Hill Professional Publishing, 1990.

Boy Erased

You are going to watch the film *Boy Erased*, which was directed by Joel Edgerton (2018).
Film posters, DVD covers and trailers provide a selected visual preview attempting to catch and arouse the potential target groups' interest to advertise and promote the film.

PRE-VIEWING: A FILM POSTER

1

Look at the film poster below. Using it as a starting point, first describe the poster and then speculate about the content and the genre of the film. Give reasons for your answers.

____

____

____

____

____

____

____

____

____

Language support

Description / Layout of a poster

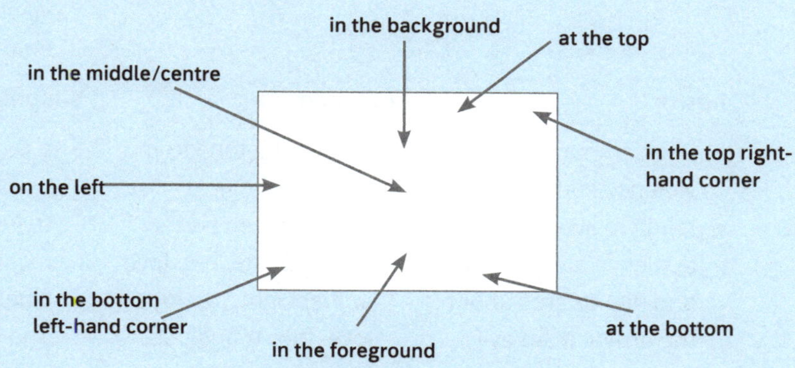

- On the film poster / In the picture I can see ... / There is / are / seems to be ... / One can see ...
- The poster shows/illustrates/depicts ...
- The field size is a close-up/medium shot/long shot ...
- The layout emphasizes ... / The layout is rather detailed/simple with ...
- The focus of attention ... / What strikes the eye is the key/main image / the image of ... taking up the most space ...
- There is a contrast between ... / A contrast is clearly recognizable/visible.

Language support

Talking about content und genre

- When looking at the film poster, I think/feel/am reminded of ... / Initially the image makes me think / gives the impression of ...
- The choice of colours supports the idea of / suggests / contributes to ...
- The film's mood and tone are reflected/illustrated by ... / It can be assumed that ... because ... / ... is a symbol of ...
- The film poster appeals to audiences that enjoy films containing dramatic tension / showing male views of the world / about protecting law and order, right and wrong / focusing on one protagonist, powerful and ready to take on the enemy ...
- The film poster depicts/shows/portrays/represents/illustrates/conveys ... which is why I believe/think ...

✓ Use the simple present tense to talk about the poster.
✓ Use the present progressive if you refer to actions in the image. (This is not applicable to verbs of perception or verbs with static meaning, e.g. *be, believe, hate, like, love, mean, notice, see, think, wish, ...*)
✓ Use specific descriptive expressions (e.g. *on the left, at the bottom, ...*).
✓ Use suitable adjectives and adverbs.
✓ Employ linking words/connectives.

Info

Some examples of genres

action	**crime**	**documentary**	**drama**
• speed action • physical stunts and chases • rescues, battles, fights, escapes, destructive crises • often standard heroes and villains (good guy – bad guy)	• high speed with some mystery • action of a criminal mastermind versus the rise and fall of sinister criminals	• non-fictional • reporting on an issue of interest	• serious and plot-driven • rounded, real-life characters, settings, situations, and stories • characterized by an intense character development and interaction • vigorous human emotions
fantasy	**horror**	**romance**	**suspense/mystery**
• imaginative and fantasy themes • fairy-tale adventures or plots from Dark Ages • magic, supernatural elements	• large amount of violence in the plot • trying to awaken audience's worst fears and nightmares about the arrival of an evil force or event • often mythical creatures, such as ghosts, vampires, and zombies	• alternating tone from happy to tragic • love between two protagonists, e.g. love at first sight, forbidden love, love triangles and love requiring great sacrifices	• a person of authority, usually a detective, trying to solve a mysterious crime • clues, investigation, and logical reasoning • constant suspense created through visual cues or unusual plot twists

PRE-VIEWING: REVISITING CINEMATOGRAPHY

In order to analyse and talk about *Boy Erased* properly you need some film specific terms and phrases. When dealing with films, camera operations and music or sound play a vital role in guiding and influencing the viewer as intended by the film-makers.

2 → **Workshop:** Analysing a feature film

Look at the most common cinematic devices that are used in films. Match the functions on the right to the given operations on the left.

I FIELD SIZE

Camera operations		Functions
A long shot	☐	1 points out sth specific about sb/sth
B full shot	☐	2 provides a complete picture of sb/sth
C medium shot	☐	3 points out a particular detail about sb/sth
D close-up shot	☐	4 presents the setting of the scene
E extreme close-up shot	☐	5 provides a closer look at sb/sth

II CAMERA MOVEMENT

Camera operations		Functions
A static shot	☐	1 horizontal/vertical movement from a static position to shift focus towards or away from sb/sth
B zooming in/out	☐	2 creates the impression of following sb/sth
C panning/tilting shot	☐	3 no movement; creates a feeling of hesitation/calmness/slowness
D tracking shot	☐	4 puts focus on something or takes focus away

III CAMERA ANGLE AND POSITION

Camera operations		Functions
A overhead shot	☐	1 creates an overall impression of the scene
B high-angle shot/bird's eye	☐	2 creates a neutral impression
C eye-level shot	☐	3 makes sb/sth seem unimportant
D low-angle shot	☐	4 represents a character's perspective
E over-the-shoulder shot	☐	5 creates the impression of being involved in a conversation
F reverse-angle shot	☐	6 usually in connection with over-the-shoulder to show the other character's reaction/side
G point-of-view shot	☐	7 sets the scene that's to come
H establishing shot	☐	8 makes sb/sth look important

IV EDITING/MONTAGE

Techniques		Functions
A fast cuts	☐	1 opens/closes an action or a scene slowly
B slow cuts	☐	2 create focus on sth specific or create calm atmosphere
C fade-in/fade-out	☐	3 intensifying an action/moment
D cross-cut	☐	4 depict action vividly
E slow motion	☐	5 focuses on contrast and thus creates suspense
F fast motion	☐	6 provides a comment on the action
G voice-over	☐	7 changing chronological order and therefore connecting/ disconnecting action/moments
H flashback/flash-forward	☐	8 focus on text and its meaning, gives additional information without adding voices or stressing the meaning of voices
I floating, superimposed text	☐	9 intensifies speed, creating the impression of change

Language support

Talking about cinematography

General phrases:

- The establishing shot of the film shows/portrays ... / ... is shown in a medium shot/(extreme) close-up / ...
- ... brings the viewer closer to ... / creates a distance between ...
- The focus is on ... in detail.
- The movement of ... is followed in a ... shot.
- The shots follow each other quickly/slowly.
- The viewer sees the character in ... / There is a close-up of the character ...
- The scene is shot from X's point of view. / ... is seen from the perspective of ...
- The director uses a long shot of the setting. / ... uses high-angle/low-angle/eye-level shots of ...
- The camera pans from left to right / tilts up/down.

Effects of cinematography:

- ... describes characters indirectly / shows a character's emotions / draws attention to sth / describes the setting / evokes a certain atmosphere ...
- ... is presented in a low-angle shot/high-angle shot, which illustrates inferiority/vulnerability/superiority/ power ...
- The point-of-view shots make the audience experience the (emotional) perspective of ...
- The close-up is used to focus attention on ... / reveals the character's feelings / makes the situation more intimate.
- ... is shown in a close-up so the viewer can see the reaction in his/her face when ...
- The over-the-shoulder shots include the viewers in the action.
- ... uses a fade-in / fade-out to ...
- The hand-held camera underlines ... / gives the scene an unsteady quality / aims for authenticity ...
- The light used in the scene is harsh/soft/bright/intense / ...
- The ... is used to focus on ... / draw attention to ... / This ... emphasizes/stresses/indicates ...
- ... is used to build (up) suspense / tension / to create a certain effect / to convey a feeling of / to create a mood to set the scene ...
- ... affects/touches the viewers ...
- ... suggests/signifies that / provides a strong contrast to / serves as an insight into ... / bridges two scenes ...

Info

Music/Sound

1. **diegetic sounds:** sounds from 'the world inside the film', e.g. conversation, a window closing, footsteps
2. **non-diegetic sounds:** sounds from 'the world outside the film', e.g. film music, sounds creating suspense
3. **voice-over** (off-camera commentary): non-diegetic information by a narrator

→ to build up suspense
→ to develop a certain mood / to create a certain atmosphere
→ to describe a character
→ to foreshadow an event

Language support

Talking about cinematography

Music/Sound:

- The music is upbeat/gloomy/aggressive/slow/fast-paced ...
- The rhythmic/background music contributes to the atmosphere of ...
- The effect of this scene is enhanced by the music. / ... contributes to the mood/atmosphere of the scene.
- The music provides an extra feeling of tension / adds to the atmosphere.
- The scene is accompanied by soft/alarming/melancholic music.
- The lyrics suggest ...

WHILE VIEWING

Characters

3 Group work

Now you are going to watch the entire film. Form groups that focus on preassigned characters and take notes while watching the film.

- Jared
- Nancy Eamons (mother)
- Marshall Eamons (father)
- Victor Sykes (camp leader)
- Brandon Ellis
- Cameron
- Sarah
- Gary

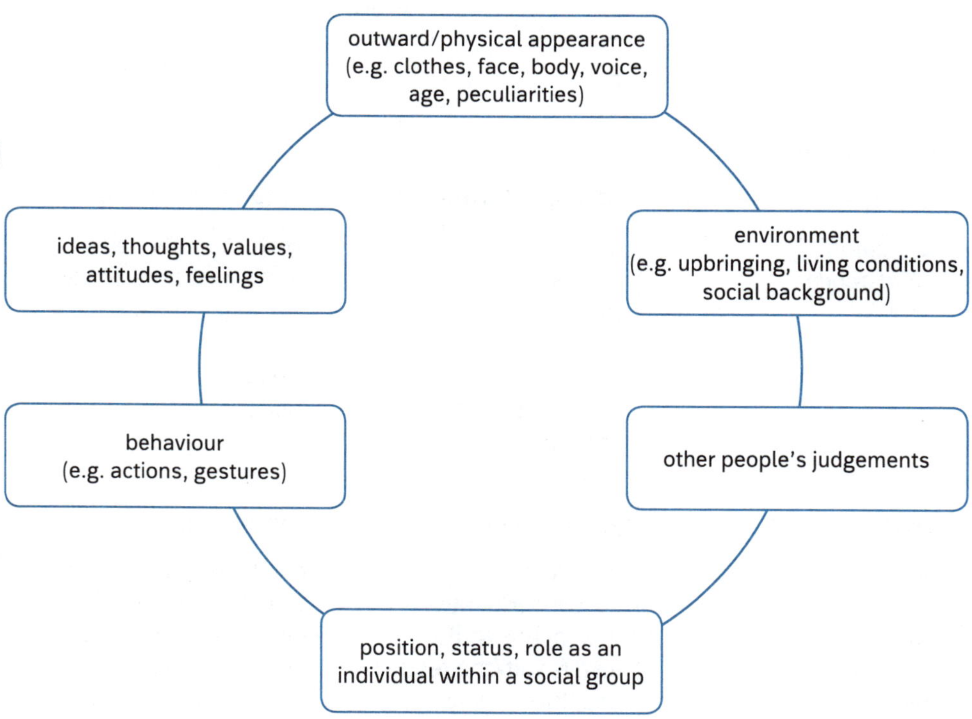

Compare your findings with classmates who have been dealing with the same character.
Design a (digital) poster and be prepared to present it to the class (→ gallery walk).

Language support

Talking about characters

General phrases:
- The main/principle character in the story is ...
- Another central character is ...
- ... is characterized/described/portrayed/depicted/presented as ... / ... proves to be ...
- As far as his/her character is concerned, it can be said that he/she is ...
- Concerning his/her character, it can be said that ... This character trait becomes apparent when ...
- ... seems to be ...
- The body language / The action reveals that ...
- His/Her statement "..." shows/proves/reveals that ... / From this one can conclude that ...
- It is quite apparent that ...
- When saying that ... he/she reveals that he/she is/feels ...
- Proof of this can be found in/when ...
- This is an example of ...
- He/She has many positive personality traits/traits of character/characteristics.
- His/Her behaviour is marked by ... He/She shows ... behaviour.
- A positive/negative aspect of his/her behaviour is ...
- He/She reacts ...
- He/She gradually develops into ... / In the course of the film he/she undergoes a development.
- ... remains unchanged.
- ... is/reacts/shows/seems to be/feels ...
- The motive/reason for his/her action ... is ...
- ... is influenced by ...
- The relationship can be described as / characterized by ...

Positive character traits			**Negative character traits**	
active affectionate ambitious brave caring charismatic charming compassionate confident	conscientious courageous dedicated glamorous honourable humble mature patriotic perseverant	proud reliable sensitive sophisticated talkative tenacious virtuous warm-hearted witty	bad-tempered cold-hearted deceitful grouchy hypocritical ignorant impolite jealous malicious narrow-minded	obnoxious old-fashioned petty-minded rude self-centred stubborn

Useful linking words

giving examples	**adding information**	**sequencing ideas**	**summarizing**
for example for instance such as	and as well as too in addition also furthermore, moreover, apart from, in addition to, besides	the former, the latter firstly, secondly, finally the first point is lastly the following last but not least	in short, in brief, to summarize, to sum up, in a nutshell, to put it in a nutshell, to conclude, in conclusion, all in all, on the whole
giving reasons	**giving a result**	**contrasting ideas**	**comparing ideas**
due to/due to the fact that owing to/owing to the fact that because/because of since/as	therefore so/consequently this means that as a result/the result is this/that is why hence/thus	but, however, although/even though, despite/despite the fact that, in spite of/in spite of the fact that, nevertheless, nonetheless, while, whereas, in contrast (to)	similarly equally likewise in the same way

Language support

relating information	reformulating	giving opinions	emphasizing facts
with regard to, with respect to, referring to, regarding, according to, when it comes to	in other words, to put it another way	in my/his/her opinion, my opinion is, I think, I believe, in my view, from my point of view, to my mind	in fact, obviously, undoubtedly, for this reason, again, fortunately, unfortunately, indeed

4 CHALLENGE → **Workshop:** Ananalysing characters → **S8:** How to improve your text

Write a characterization of your assigned character.

Practices of conversion therapy

5

a) While watching the film, take notes on how the conversion therapy program Love In Action works. Focus on the following aspects:

Love In Action	
Circumstances	*staff wear uniforms and use walkie-talkies, …*
Rules	*no mobile phones, no talking about the therapy with parents, …*
Routines and methods	*genograms, …*
Forms of therapy	*12 days (from 9:00 am to 5:00 pm), …*

b) Comment on the emotional, psychological and physical abuse as carried out by Love In Action.

6 CHALLENGE → **S16:** Checklist: Analysis of a film scene → **Workshop:** Analysing a feature film

Analyse how cinematography and film music contribute to the depiction and atmosphere of Love In Action (0:04:45–0:08:35). (You can use "Revisiting cinematography" on pp. 83–85.)

7

John Smid (cf. task 11 on p. 75, **Webcode** DSW-73654-03) reports that conversion therapy practices are similar to Alcoholics Anonymous (AA). Look at the Twelve Steps of the AA program and compare them to your findings about the conversion therapy Love In Action.

1. We admitted we were powerless over alcohol – that our lives had become unmanageable.
2. Came to believe that a Power greater than ourselves could restore us to sanity.
3. Made a decision to turn our will and our lives over to the care of God as we understood Him.
4. Made a searching and fearless moral inventory of ourselves.
5. Admitted to God, to ourselves and to another human being the exact nature of our wrongs.
6. Were entirely ready to have God remove all these defects of character.
7. Humbly asked Him to remove our shortcomings.
8. Made a list of all persons we had harmed, and became willing to make amends to them all.
9. Made direct amends to such people wherever possible, except when to do so would injure them or others.
10. Continued to take personal inventory and when we were wrong promptly admitted it.
11. Sought through prayer and meditation to improve our conscious contact with God as we understood Him, praying only for knowledge of His will for us and the power to carry that out.
12. Having had a spiritual awakening as the result of these steps, we tried to carry this message to alcoholics and to practice these principles in all our affairs.

Portrayals of homosexuality

8

Watch the scene about Jared outing himself again (0:40:23–0:50:09).

a) Outline the plot.
b) Examine how the plot is supported by cinematography. Pay close attention to the use of light and shadow.
c) CHALLENGE Why does Jared finally out himself? In class, discuss whether the trauma of the rape confirmed Jared's idea that homosexuality was sinful and destructive and might have been a catalyst.

9

Watch the scene at Dr. Muldoon's office again (0:50:12–0:52:01).

a) Read Dr. Muldoon's diagnosis below and state why she is "in a bit of a bind".
b) Explain what Dr. Muldoon is aiming at.
c) Comment on why Jared seems unable to take her advisory diagnosis.

> "Your father's asked me to take some of your blood. He wants me to check for testosterone levels. I'm in a bit of a bind here, Jared, and I said this to your mother too. Now, I'm a religious woman, there's no question, but I have also been to medical school. And, well, you can say that I hold science in one hand and God in the other, and that is not always an easy balance. And I know that everybody would like for me to say otherwise and send you down to the pharmacy for a pill that would magically fix you, but that's not going to happen. But I'm going to take your blood, and I know what it's going to show me. That you are a perfectly normal, very healthy teenage boy. Jared, it's not my place to tell you that your parents are wrong, but let's say that they are wrong. I understand your father signed you up for a program next month. Whatever happens next, it is still your choice. It may not feel that way, but it is. You're eighteen. Do you have anything that you'd like to say to me? Any questions?"

10

Watch the scene with Gary giving advice to Jared again (1:09:16–1:11:01).

a) State what Gary advises Jared to do.
b) Imagine you are Gary. Write a blog post for the website "Survivors of Conversion Therapy". Report on your experiences with Love In Action and give advice on how to "survive" to people who are obliged to take part in conversion therapy. → **S7:** Checklist: Writing a blog post
c) CHALLENGE Do you think conversion therapy has worked for anyone doing it? Discuss in class.

11

Read and rewatch Sarah's and Gary's moral inventory scenes.

Moral inventory	
Sarah (0:26:50–0:28:27)	**Gary (0:54:45–0:55:51)**
"I would look at other girls in the changing rooms before gym and in the showers. My biggest sin is one that I am also thankful for, because it has led me to Love in Action. […] I had run away from my uncle's house and stayed with some girls I knew whose parents were away. It was there that I finally acted on my homosexual thoughts. […] I let a girl touch my … kiss m-my … my vagina … […] … and put her fingers inside me, and I did the same. I renounce these sinful thoughts and actions, and ask God to forgive me all these things."	"Dear Heavenly Father, today I ask your forgiveness for my sins. For a year, we lived together under the cover of being roommates. But in reality, the whole time, I was committing the sin of sodomy. And then my family discovered the truth and brought me back to my senses. They helped me realize that I was fooling myself. That I was being fooled. That I was seduced into a life of sin by all sorts of sinful people. And I knew in my heart that I had forsaken Jesus for Satan. But now … I am awake to my sins. I'm enlightened. I'm here with all of you. And I am disgusted at the person that I once was. I want to ask God for his forgiveness, and I want to thank all of you guys, especially you, Mr. Sykes, for helping me get back on the path to righteousness."

a) Outline each moral inventory.
b) Compare Sarah's and Gary's moral inventory.
c) CHALLENGE Imagine you are either Sarah or Gary. After having presented your moral inventory, you decide to put down your thoughts and feelings by writing a diary entry. Write one diary entry reflecting on your moral inventory.
- Start with "Dear Diary, …".
- Write in the first person.
- Be honest and reflective.
- Ponder on and express your feelings.

12

Watch the scenes with Brandon Ellis again (0:22:14–0:26:16).
a) When is a man a man? Examine and outline how concepts of masculinity are portrayed by the program Love In Action.
b) Discuss the validity of masculinity as portrayed by Love In Action.

13 Group work CHOOSE

Form groups and choose one of the following tasks. Present your results to the class.
a) Rewatch the scene where Mr. Sykes advises Jared to stay in the program for a year instead of going to college (0:52:02–0:54:45).
- Explain why Mr. Sykes thinks that college is not a good idea at all.
- Research the book titles from the reading list that Mr. Sykes names. Why does Mr. Sykes consider these books dangerous for Jared?

OR

b) Rewatch the scene where Jared goes jogging in the evening, destroys an advertising sign and swears (0:57:30–0:58:32).
- Outline the scene.
- Explain what is going on inside Jared and why he is so enraged.

OR

c) Rewatch Jared's encounter with Brandon in the bathroom (1:07:40–1:09:15).
- Outline what is being said and done. Comment on the humiliation carried out by Brandon in this scene.
- Do some research on gay bashing. Evaluate whether Brandon's words and actions can be considered to be gay bashing.

OR

d) "Love In Action meets exorcism": Rewatch the scenes where Cameron is being harmed physically (1:13:01–1:15:50).
- Analyse the scenes.
- CHALLENGE Comment on the violence used by Love In Action and its members as well as by Cameron's family.

OR

e) Rewatch Jared's attempt to deliver his moral inventory (1:19:00–1:26:22).
- Summarize the scenes around Jared's moral inventory and his intention to quit the program and go home by outlining reasons why Jared is getting more and more angry, frustrated and fearful.
- Examine how the intensity of these scenes is underscored by cinematographic and musical means (cf. "Revisiting cinematography" on pp. 83–85).

Homosexuality as God's test?

14 Pair work

In Xavier's studio room Jared talks about Job (1:02:25–1:03:01):

> "I imagine I'm him sometimes. And that God and the Devil are having a bet over me. That one day God will let me in on the experiment he was having to test me."

Read the information on Job and discuss if Jared's comparison is fitting.

Info

Job

Job is a figure from the Bible. A book of the Old Testament named after him tells his story: In essence, Job's story says that you should keep your faith in God even in difficult times.
Job is a wealthy man who has a big family and lives a good life. He firmly believes in God and wants to obey him unconditionally. One day Satan speaks to God and claims that Job only serves God because of his blessed life and God's protection; if God stopped protecting Job, Job would stop serving him. God is certain that Job will remain devout, so he allows the Devil to test Job.
A lot of terrible things happen: Job loses his livestock and all of his possessions, his servants and even his children die, and Job himself suffers from bad pain. Job is desperate and complains about his suffering, but despite all that he does not lose his faith in God. As a reward for his faithfulness, Job finally gets back prosperity and health; God gives him a new family and a long and happy life.

Time and symbolism

15

Jared's hand in the wind during car rides is a reoccurring symbol in the film.

a) Read the information on the symbolism of wind below.

b) Rewatch the following scenes:
0:04:05–0:04:25 | 0:13:06–0:17:06 | 0:55:52–0:57:07 | 1:32:11–1:33:31 | 1:42:46–1:43:46

c) Analyse this reoccurring symbol against the background of your knowledge about the plot.

Info

Wind

Wind surrounds people and it is also in them as breath. Breath means life. Through wind and draughts, people can hear vibrations and perceive smells.
Whoever tries to grasp at wind reaches into a void. Wind is volatile and can appear in different forms: welcomed as a mild breeze on hot summer days or feared as the persistent force of a hurricane.
Wind is not only a meteorological phenomenon, but also a supernatural manifestation: the intentions of the gods. On the one hand, wind can be unpredictable and unreliable – on the other hand, it has tangible effects despite its invisibility. In many cultures, wind is understood as the breath of God. Wind is also associated with indomitable powers. In the Old Testament the Spirit of God is spoken of as "ruach", the breath of wind. At the creation of man, God breathed into man the breath of life.

16

a) Read the information on screen vs. plot duration below.
b) Analyse how in the film the plot duration has been compressed to the screen duration. You may rewatch the following scenes:
0:03:24–0:04:00 | 0:30:18–0:52:02 | 1:00:25–1:04:12 | 1:16:35–1:18:03 | 1:30:58–1:31:06

Info

Screen duration vs. plot duration

Screen duration is the time that passes until a story is fully told. For a film it is simply its length or its time duration, so for *Boy Erased* it is 110 minutes.
The time that passes within that story is called **plot duration**. For example, from Jared's time at Love In Action to living in New York City: About five years of Jared's life (5 years = 2,628,000 minutes = plot duration) are told in 110 minutes (= screen duration).
Usually, films compress the plot duration, i.e. it is much shorter than the time span in which the story takes place. This is possible with the help of editing: Employing fades, time lapse and slow motion, directors and editors can create a new, cinematic time within the framework of editing – beyond the possibilities of the camera. Here are some examples:

fade-in / fade-out	If a film frame fades in smoothly from darkening to the first film frame, the fade-in opens our field of vision to something that was already there before and in which the action will now take part. Conversely, the slowly darkening image as a fade-out symbolizes the passage of time in a shot.
crossfade	A crossfade merges two shots together: The previous shot fades – and the following shot appears almost simultaneously.
flashback	A flashback is the insertion of a scene into a storyline which shows earlier events. Flashbacks can be memories, but also explanations for the viewer. With a flashback, the viewer gets a head start in knowledge compared to the characters appearing in the film.
flash-forward	A flash-forward is a short scene in which the action jumps ahead to the future. It takes a narrative forward in time from the current point of the story.
jump cut	A jump cut is an unusual alternative to time compression. It is a cut between two images that are identical in terms of camera distance and framing, but make a jump in the action.
durative time lapse	In the case of durative time lapse, time sequences that have no connection with the characters in the plot are cinematically condensed, for example the change of seasons or the growth of plants.

Info

iterative time lapse	Iterative time lapse shows sequences of images of characters doing recurring, regular activities – such as driving to work every day: in this example, the change of clothes indicates that not one, but several car trips to work are shown.
cinematic time lapse	Cinematic time lapse can be visualized by speeding up or slowing down the time depicted.
music	Music may be employed for connecting different scenes that occur over time as a musical montage; a piece of music may help the viewer to understand the totality of all the scenes in a montage, and what is trying to be expressed.

POST-VIEWING

17 CHALLENGE

Research the real people represented in the film *Boy Erased* and compare the film characters with the real, authentic people and their stories.

- Jared Eamons – Garrard Conley
- Victor Sykes – John Smid

Garrard Conley and Lucas Hedges (as Jared Eamons)

18 CHOOSE

a) Rewatch the scene where Jared's father asks for information about Henry Wallace to take (legal) action (0:42:54–0:44:34). Imagine you are the script writer. Develop and write a short screenplay about Henry being confronted with allegations against him.

OR

b) **Pair work**
After Jared's dramatic leave from the camp, it remains hidden from the viewer what happens at Love In Action after Nancy "rescued" her son. Discuss with a partner what camp leader Mr. Sykes might do to calm down the situation and what he might do to Cameron, who helped Jared. Imagine you are the script writer. Develop and write a screenplay.

Info

How to write a screenplay

- Write your screenplay based on what you know about the characters and the plot of the film as well as plausible deductions.
- Before you start writing, answer the following questions: Who? What? When? Where? Why?
- Indicate the setting, camera operations, action lines (the equivalent of stage directions in a theatre play) and props.

19

After Jared has heard about Cameron's suicide (1:29:20–1:30:45), he retires to his room. As Jared loves writing, he might write down his feelings in a diary. Imagine you are Jared. Write his diary entry.

- Start with "Dear Diary, ...".
- Write in the first person.
- Be honest and reflective.
- Ponder on and express your feelings.

20

After having dealt with Joel Edgerton's film *Boy Erased* in detail, write a film review for an online audience. Use the following guidelines to structure your text.

Info

How to write a film review

A film review offers information on a film. It is usually a recommendation for a film or informs its readers why it might not be worth watching.

- Start with a catchy introduction in which you give essential information about the film (title, director, genre, release date, actors, characters, setting and plot).
- Then, give a brief summary of what the film is about, but avoid spoilers.
- Afterwards, state your personal impression of the film.
- Finally, point out the purpose of the film and come up with a convincing conclusion as to why the reader should or should not watch the film.

Language support

Writing a film review

Useful phrases:

- The film "..." is a drama/action film/thriller/...
- The film was directed/produced by ... and released in ...
- The film was well-directed by ...
- Starring ... (actor's name)
- The main character is played ...
- ... is absolutely remarkable as ...
- The acting is remarkable/convincing/too melodramatic ...
- The film won ... / was awarded ...

Characters/Plot:

- The main character is called ...
- The story is about/deals with/focuses on ...
- The film tells the story of ...
- The film opens/begins with ...
- As the story continues/unfolds/develops ...
- The plot is multi-dimensional/complicated/thrilling/captivating / arouses curiosity / is full of tension ...
- The plot has a surprising twist. / The plot is incoherent/mediocre/appalling ...
- One of the best moments in the film is when ...
- It's a non-linear/fragmented narrative.
- The characters show an exceptional performance when ...
- The characters are believable/shallow/unconvincing ...

Setting:

- It is set in ...
- The story takes place in / unfolds in ...
- The film begins in ...
- The film creates a ... atmosphere/mood ...

Cinematography:

- The camera work is impressive/spectacular/unrealistic/confusing ...
- The camera operations draw attention to ...
- The special effects are stunning/impressive/poor/amateurish ...
- The music is profound/clichéd/conveys a ... atmosphere ...
- The music underlines emotions/connects scenes ...

Opinion

- I believe ...
- He/She does a very god job as ...
- I (highly/strongly/definitely) recommend/don't recommend this film because ...
- A 'must-see'/box-office success/failure! / Don't miss it!
- A very impressive portrayal of ...
- On a scale of 1–10, I give this film a ...
- The best/worst thing is ...
- If you like ... this film is for you.
- The film is a worthwhile watch. / I'm afraid the film is a complete waste of time and money. Only watch this film if you have plenty of time to spare.
- ... is well worth seeing / not to be missed / a truly great piece of filmmaking.
- The film is exciting/realistic/over-complicated/confusing/far-fetched ...
- The film is thought-provoking/touching/moving ...

Coming of age

1

Read the information about the coming-of-age genre below. Transfer the given information into a suitable form of visualization (e.g. graphic organizer, mind map/concept map, flow chart, plot diagram, fish-bone graphic, etc.).

Info

Coming of age – or: The crises of adolescence

The transition between childhood and adulthood, becoming an adult or entering maturity, is referred to as 'coming of age'.
Coming-of-age as a genre refers to literature and films in which older children and adolescents[1] as the protagonists encounter for the first time fundamental issues of growing up or intense emotions that call for maturing[2] socially and psychologically. The focus is on the confrontation with the adult world, the parental home, school and society. The plot usually revolves around family, social or individual conflicts, sexuality, gender roles, rebellion, opinion formation, and other moral as well as emotional challenges that young people face during puberty. The protagonist will encounter[3] loss or discovery, or an internal or external conflict, making him/her suffer from arduous[4] trials and misfortunes and personal development, change and growth. However, these crucial[5] experiences will eventually lead to life-altering adulthood despite scarification[6]. The protagonist will find himself/herself clashing with their traditional culture and societal standards while progressing. Courses of self-discovery, identity formation and emancipation are characteristic of this genre. It is the protagonist's psychological or sometimes even physical journey from being a child to being an adult: from naive to wise, from idealist to realist, and from immature to mature. Dialogues and emotional responses are more in focus than the action itself, and often the story is told in the form of flashbacks. Both provide deep insights into the protagonist.

The typical plot pattern of a coming-of-age story is as follows: At the beginning, the exposition, the protagonist is in a childhood stage. He/She is young, immature, naive, and feels alienated[7] and alone. As his/her story proceeds, the action rises to a conflict. Here the protagonist encounters a challenge or a problem. The plot continues with the protagonist's struggle to overcome his/her challenge. At one turning point, comparable to a climax, there is a sudden realization of the truth about himself/herself or the world, an "epiphany"[8]. The protagonist makes a tough decision regarding his/her problem and starts changing because of this decision. With falling action comes the story's conclusion, in which the protagonist displays evidence of change. He/She has found a sense of belonging or self-realization reaching maturity. He/She is now seen as different or changed and the significance of the change is revealed. The protagonist finally enters the adulthood stage.
Because of the universal, relatable and dramatic nature of these coming-of-age narrative motifs, the genre belongs to the most popular genres of literary fiction. Mark Twain's *The Adventures of Tom Sawyer*, the *Harry Potter* series by J.K. Rowling, Stephenie Meyer's *Twilight*, or Lois Lowry's *The Giver* are some prominent examples of coming-of-age stories: fictional texts in which the process of growing up is portrayed.

Annotations

1 **adolescent** = a young person who is developing from a child into an adult
2 to **mature** = to develop emotionally and start to behave like a sensible adult
3 to **encounter** = to experience something, especially something unpleasant or difficult, while you are trying to do something else
4 **arduous** = involving a lot of effort and energy, especially over a period of time
5 **crucial** = extremely important or necessary
6 **scarification** = the result of scarifying (making small cuts in somebody's skin), a scratch or scratches
7 **alienated** = feeling of not belonging and being separated
8 **epiphany** = a sudden and surprising moment of understanding

COMING OF AGE IN *BOY ERASED*

2

Examine in what way the film *Boy Erased* can be seen as a coming-of-age story by focusing on and exemplifying Jared's journey through conversion therapy and ending up as a journalist.

3 CHOOSE → **S8:** How to improve your text

Right at the beginning of the film, Jared states (0:02:08–0:02:15):

> "I wish none of this had ever happened. But sometimes, I thank God that it did."

Using this quote, give a two-minute presentation **OR** write an argumentative essay in which you justify why *Boy Erased* can be classified as a coming-of-age story.

4

The German title of the film *Boy Erased* is "Der verlorene Sohn" ("The Lost Son"), which is an allusion to the Parable of the Prodigal Son in the New Testament of the Bible, appearing in Luke 15:11–32.

a) Research the Parable of the Prodigal Son and outline it.
b) Compare the biblical parable to the film.
c) CHALLENGE Write a blog post in which you make a reasoned case for the film title that you think is more appropriate. Justify your opinion. → **S7:** Checklist: Writing a blog post

Sexual diversity – Tolerance and discrimination

MEDIATION: CONVERSION THERAPY IN GERMANY

1 → **Workshop:** Mediation → **S19:** How to improve your mediation skills → **S8:** How to improve your text

At the end of the film *Boy Erased*, we get to know that Jared publishes articles on conversion therapy. Imagine that Jared has asked his international online community to help him with his research on gay conversion therapy in other countries. Read the following interview from Deutschlandfunk Kultur on a new German law banning conversion therapy. Write an e-mail to Jared in which you explain to him what the German law prohibits and why.

Gesetz gegen „Homoheiler"– Ein Meilenstein für Deutschland

Markus Kowalski im Gespräch mit Stephan Karkowsky • 07.05.2020

„Homoheilern" soll das Handwerk gelegt werden. Der Bundestag stimmt über ein Verbot von „Konversionstherapien" ab, die Homosexuelle oder Transgender „umdrehen" sollen. Ein gutes Signal, findet der Journalist Markus Kowalski.

Stephan Karkowsky: Der Bundestag will heute über ein Gesetz abstimmen, das sogenannte Konversionstherapien erschweren soll, also Angebote von selbst ernannten „Homoheilern", die Sexualität als Krankheit betrachten und deshalb behandeln wollen. Der Lesben- und Schwulenverband kritisiert das Gesetz als nicht weitgehend genug. Über die Details sprechen möchte ich mit dem Journalisten Markus Kowalski, der das Thema seit Jahren verfolgt. Was genau wird heute verboten und was bleibt erlaubt?

Markus Kowalski: Es wird verboten, dass man Homosexuellen und Transgendern anbietet, geheilt zu werden, wie auch immer das passieren soll, also heterosexuell zu werden oder cisgeschlechtlich zu werden. Das heißt, zum Beispiel Transgendern anzubieten, wieder in das von Geburt an biologische Geschlecht zurückzukehren.

Darf man das, im juristischen Sinne, verbieten?

Karkowsky: Ist denn nur das Angebot verboten und die Werbung dafür?

Kowalski: Genau, es ist beides verboten. Zum einen ist es verboten, dafür zu werben, dafür droht einem 30.000 Euro Geldstrafe. Und wenn man die Therapie wirklich durchführt, dann droht einem bis zu einem Jahr Haft. Das ist schon eine ordentliche Abschreckung, die da heute im Gesetz beschlossen wird.

Karkowsky: Die Haft betrifft diese Pseudo-„Homoheiler", aber nicht verboten werden die Pseudobehandlungen generell für Erwachsene, die sich freiwillig einer solchen Therapie unterziehen wollen. Warum nicht?

Kowalski: Da gibt es juristische Fragen, also Detailfragen, ob man das überhaupt verbieten kann, weil natürlich trotzdem jeder Erwachsene mit seinem Leben machen kann, was er will. Aber in dem Gesetz gibt es eben diese folgende Regelung, dass, wenn man sagt, okay, Erwachsene dürfen trotzdem nicht diese Konversionstherapie bekommen, wenn ihr Wille beeinträchtigt ist, das heißt, wenn sie genötigt wurden oder gezwungen wurden, das zu tun.

Ich glaube, das ist eine ganz intelligente Lösung, weil genau das ja in der Gesellschaft passiert. Homosexuelle werden dazu gezwungen oder genötigt, sich anzupassen, heterosexuell zu werden oder sich zu verhalten, und deswegen ist diese Ausnahme trotzdem im Gesetz eingebaut.

[...]

Karkowsky: Wie groß ist denn das Problem überhaupt, dass der Bundestag heute da ein eigenes Gesetz zu beschließen muss, wie viele gehen diesen selbst ernannten Homoheilern auf den Leim, mit dem Versprechen, Schwule und Lesben angeblich heilen zu können? Weiß man das?

Kowalski: Ja, es gab eine Studie von der Bundesstiftung Magnus Hirschfeld, die sich jetzt damit beschäftigt hat im Zuge dieses Verfahrens, die hat gesagt, sie schätzen, ungefähr 1000 Betroffene pro Jahr gibt es in Deutschland. Das heißt, das sind vor allem Heranwachsende, Jugendliche oder junge Erwachsene in den religiösen Gemeinden, die da aufwachsen und in diesen Strukturen verstrickt sind und da einfach beeinflusst werden in ihrem Heranwachsen und da sich nicht frei äußern können, sich nicht frei zu ihrer sexuellen Orientierung bekennen können.

Depressionen bis hin zu Selbstmord

Karkowsky: Nun weiß man ja, dass diese Pseudotherapien nicht funktionieren, da könnte man sagen, na, lasst die doch machen, oder gibt es Probleme bei Leuten, die die durchgeführt haben?

Kowalski: Das Problem ist, dass zum einen für die Betroffenen das ganz schwierig ist, weil die Betroffenen ja einem enormen Druck ausgesetzt werden, was zu machen, was sie nicht sind, also als lesbische Frau plötzlich auf Männer zu stehen. Das ist natürlich extrem belastend und führt bei den Betroffenen zum einen zu einer Angst, aber auch zu Depressionen bis hin zum Selbstmord, dafür gibt es immer wieder Beispiele. Das führt natürlich auch in unserem Land zu einer Ausgrenzung und zu einem vergifteten gesellschaftlichen Klima, dass man eben zulässt, dass Leute diese falschen Theorien verbreiten und sagen, Homosexualität sei krank.

Karkowsky: Sie haben das Thema lange begleitet jetzt, jahrelang als Journalist mit Artikeln immer wieder auf das Problem aufmerksam gemacht. Das Gesetz, so wie es jetzt verabschiedet werden soll, ist das für Sie okay?

Kowalski: Ja, ich glaube, dieses Gesetz ist wirklich ein Meilenstein für dieses Land. Wir dürfen nicht vergessen, dass die wichtigen Errungenschaften für die queere Community, also für die Lesben, Schwulen, Bisexuellen und Transgender, dass die alle schon in den letzten Jahren kamen: 2017 die Ehe für alle, die dritte Geschlechtsoption für Intersexuelle, das sind wichtige Meilensteine, und heute kommt einer dazu, weil das einfach ein wichtiges Zeichen ist, dass diese Gesellschaft sagt, dieses Land sagt, wir wollen diese Konversionstherapie nicht, wir wollen dieses Klima des Hasses nicht, sondern wir wollen auch die queere Community schützen und entsprechend abschreckende Strafen in diesem Gesetz einbauen.

Der Bundestag hat am Donnerstag, 7. Mai 2020, den Gesetzentwurf der Bundesregierung „zum Schutz vor Konversionsbehandlungen" in der vom Gesundheitsausschuss geänderten Fassung angenommen. CDU/CSU, SPD und FDP stimmten für den Gesetzentwurf, die übrigen Fraktionen enthielten sich, es gab eine Gegenstimme aus der AfD-Fraktion. Unser Gespräch war bereits am Morgen gelaufen, bevor diese Entscheidung der Bundestagsabgeordneten am Abend fiel. Nähere Informationen über die Abstimmung finden Sie auf der Webseite des Deutschen Bundestages.

TOLERANCE AND DISCRIMINATION IN *BOY ERASED*

2

Throughout the film, Nancy Eamons, Jared's mother, undergoes a development: She finds her voice and emancipates herself. Outline her development using a flow chart.
You may rewatch the following scenes:
0:03:24–0:04:00 | 0:04:34–0:05:55 | 0:19:35–0:22:06 | 0:40:12–0:42:41 | 0:44:57–0:46:03 | 0:46:55–0:49:20 | 0:55:52–0:57:07 | 0:58:32–1:00:05 | 1:24:39–1:28:18 | 1:32:11–1:34:50 | 1:36:43–1:37:37

Mediation

3 → **Workshop:** Mediation → **S19:** How to improve your mediation skills → **S8:** How to improve your text

In the film, the viewer can see some of the articles Jared has written. Read the article from the German online magazine *ZEITjUNG* below. Use the given information to write one of Jared's articles ("My mother became my personal ally"). Explain what an ally is and illustrate on the basis of Nancy's actions and statements in the film in what way Jared's mother became his ally.

Was ist ein Ally?

11/08/2020 / By Salomé Kofler

Gerade im Zusammenhang mit der #blacklivesmatter-Bewegung ist der Begriff Ally in letzter Zeit immer wieder gefallen. Aber auch in der LGBTQA+-Community kennt man den Begriff. Aber woher kommt der Begriff eigentlich und was heißt er denn jetzt ganz genau? Denn hinter dem Wort „Ally" steckt viel mehr als nur ein*e Verbündete*r.

Was ist denn nun ein Ally?

Der Begriff Ally kommt aus dem Englischen und bedeutet direkt übersetzt so viel wie „Verbündete*r". Damit sind Menschen gemeint, die ihre Privilegien nutzen, um Minderheiten zu unterstützen. Sie verbünden sich also mit einer diskriminierten Gruppe, obwohl sie selbst kein Teil davon sind. Bekannt ist der Begriff vor allem in der LGBTQA+-Szene und durch die #blacklivesmatter-Bewegung. Ein Ally der LGBTQA+-Community nutzt zum Beispiel seine vorteilhaftere Position als hetero- und cisnormatives Individuum, um anderen Geschlechtsidentitäten zu helfen, in der Gesellschaft anerkannt zu werden.

Wer kann ein Ally sein?

Prinzipiell kann jede*r, der*die möchte und genug Bereitschaft zeigt, ein Ally sein. Allerdings geht es eben darum, diskriminierte Gruppen aktiv zu unterstützen, nur darüber zu reden, dass Unterdrückung falsch ist, reicht nicht. Um ein Ally zu sein, kann man logischerweise auch nicht selbst zur diskriminierten Gruppe gehören, mit der man sich verbünden möchte. In der Regel besitzt man eine vorteilhaftere Position in der Gesellschaft, die man gegen Ungerechtigkeit einsetzt.

Was genau macht ein Ally?

Verständnis und Mitleid zeigen ist schön und wichtig, das allein macht einen Ally allerdings noch nicht aus. Es ist ausschlaggebend, dass von selbst die Initiative ergriffen wird, um eine Minderheit zu unterstützen. Man kämpft den Kampf gegen die Ungerechtigkeit, als ob es sein eigener wäre. Aktiv statt passiv sein ist also ein wichtiger Punkt. Ein Ally setzt sich nicht nur für Gerechtigkeit ein, sondern akzeptiert, dass er*sie als privilegierte Mehrheit ein Teil des Problems sein kann und geht bewusst dagegen vor, indem er*sie diese Privilegien nutzt, um Menschen mit einer schwächeren Position zu helfen. Privilegiert sein heißt in dem Fall übrigens nicht, besonders reich zu sein oder ein einfaches Leben zu haben, sondern eine bestimmte Art von Benachteiligung aufgrund struktureller Ungleichheiten nie zu erleben. Ein Ally setzt sich regelmäßig mit aktuellen Themen auseinander und bleibt so gesellschaftskritisch.

Wie kannst du ein guter Ally werden?

Um ein guter Ally zu sein, muss man bereit sein, mit anderen und für andere zu handeln, um Unterdrückung endgültig zu beenden und Gleichheit zu schaffen. Für einen guten Ally gibt es einige Richtlinien, an die man sich halten kann. Zum einen sollte man sich über verschiedene Identitäten und Erfahrungen weiterbilden, die marginalisierte Gruppen gemacht haben (können). Zum anderen sollte man sich seine eigenen Vorurteile immer wieder bewusst machen und auch unangenehme Erkenntnisse reflektieren, um gegen unterbewusste und diskriminierende Ansichten vorgehen zu können. Aktives Engagement gegen Benachteiligung und Ungleichheit sind unerlässlich. Das heißt eben nicht nur, dagegen zu reden, wenn sich jemand rassistisch oder homophob äußert, sondern auch ohne Anstoß von außen selbst Dinge in die Hand zu nehmen. Man muss bereit sein, große persönliche, aber auch soziale, institutionelle und gesellschaftliche Veränderungen zu schaffen. [...]

Woher kommt der Begriff Ally?

Ursprünglich aus dem Militär übernommen wurde der Begriff von der LGBTQA+-Szene für Menschen, die sie unterstützen, selbst aber nicht Teil der Community sind und deshalb nicht diese Art von Diskriminierung erfahren haben. Mittlerweile ist der Begriff aber auch vielen Menschen bekannt durch #blacklivesmatter, besonders in Amerika hat sich der Ausdruck etabliert, aber auch im deutschsprachigen Raum wird er immer mehr genutzt. [...]

4

Read the information on tolerance vs. acceptance below.

Info

Tolerance vs. acceptance

To **tolerate** someone or something means to have a fair and objective attitude towards people that differ from you in terms of sexual orientation, religious beliefs, nationality, race, etc. You neither want to harm them nor want to be close friends with them. Tolerance can be seen as the most basic step to a functional society as it implies that you can live with a certain circumstance. It is possible to tolerate something or someone without accepting it or them.

To **accept** someone or something goes one step further and needs tolerance as a basis. It means to welcome or even endorse the reality of differences without having any intentions to change it. It can be described as an act of assenting: You cannot only live with a certain circumstance, but you even judge it favourably.

5

a) Using your knowledge from the info box above, draw a developmental line for Marshall Eamons, Jared's father. Show if and when he rejects, tolerates or accepts Jared's sexual orientation. Support your ideas with examples from the film (situations, gestures, etc.).

b) Discuss your results in class.

The development of Jared's father in *Boy Erased*

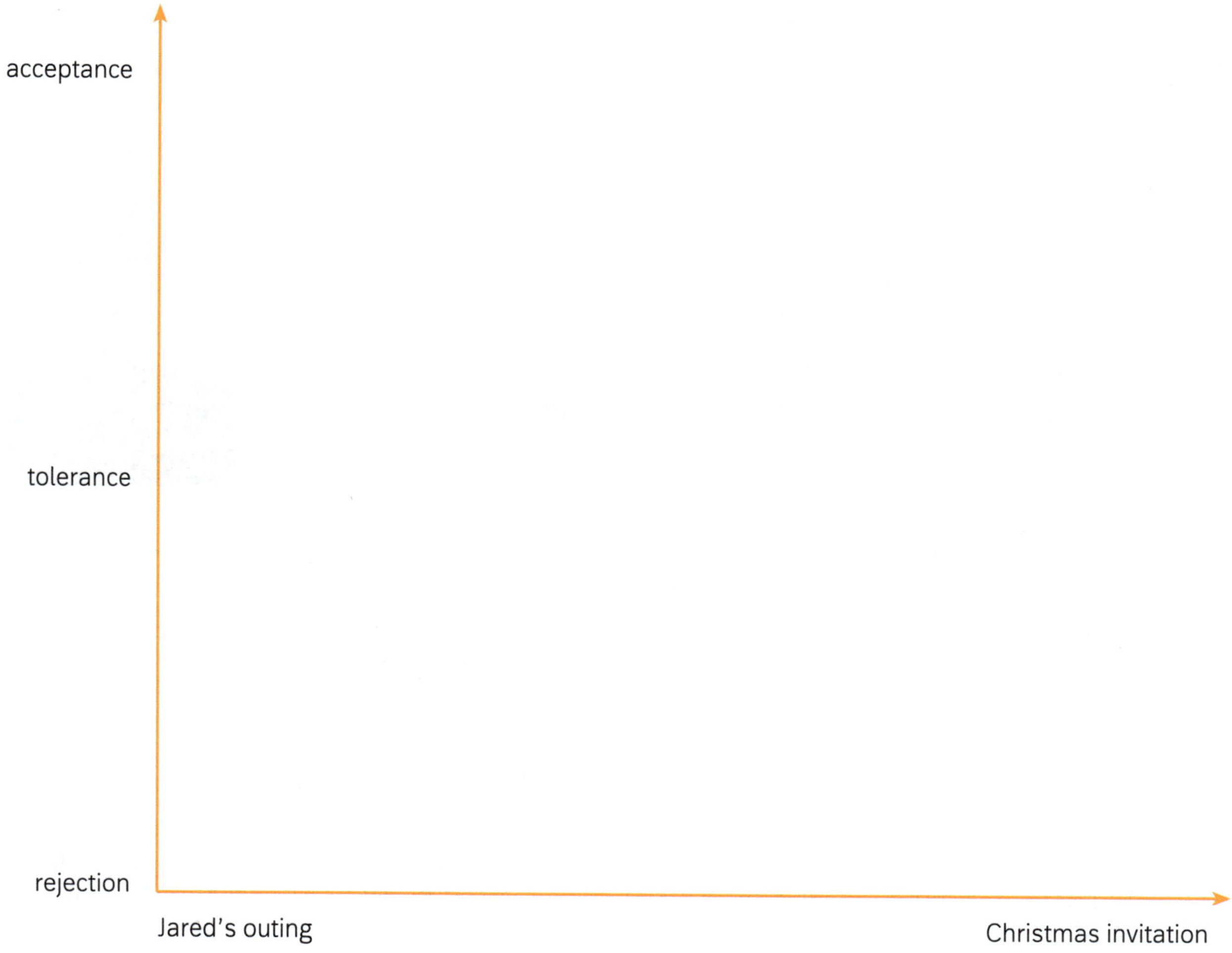

Examples from the film:

PRE-READING

1

Read the title and the PREMEDIATION. Speculate on what the play will be about.

2

a) Read the article about the dramatist Jasmine Lee-Jones.

b) Find out more about her:

- age
- family background
- motivation for writing the play
- ideals
- personal experiences with theatre
- ...

Jasmine Lee-Jones interview: I want people to come to the theatre like they watch Netflix

by Jessie Thompson

[...] Jasmine Lee-Jones's debut play, exploring female friendship, cultural appropriation and the internet, became one of the most talked-about plays of the year after a triumphant run at the Royal Court, picking up a trail of awards and an ecstatic stream of social media appreciation. [...]

It's immediately obvious when talking to Lee-Jones IRL, [...] that she is a deep and impressive thinker, often pausing for several seconds before she answers a question. [...] Born in North London, Lee-Jones became interested in theatre because of a strong connection she felt with words and language. "I always wanted to read things out loud," she says. "When I found theatre, I started to realise: oh, you can do a job where you're actually paid to speak words aloud, to really interrogate language." [...]

The play's text is written in gifs, online acronyms, merging the IRL-world with the social media-sphere. It's the most original and successful way any writer has ever managed to capture the internet on stage, but Lee-Jones didn't do it on purpose – she just wanted it to feel real. "I think theatre can sometimes feel quite isolating like, oh, this is for someone else. We have a prestige about theatre and what should be on stage, like it's just for Shakespeare. And then you put something in from the internet that feels very casual and personal to people, and people are willing to give you more license," she says.

[...] The online reaction to seven methods made it clear that the play was reaching new, more diverse audiences, something that matters greatly to Lee-Jones. "I want people to come to the theatre like they watch Netflix," she says. "I like watching reality TV and all of that as much as the next person. But one thing I find super interesting about TV is everyone will watch good, really thoroughly written, well-plotted TV. [...] But when there's something really good in theatre on, people still feel like it's not for them. There's a universality to TV and film that theatre just hasn't created yet. It's still like, oh, it's meant for those people."

Having been nurtured as a writer by the Royal Court from the age of 17, Lee-Jones has always felt more comfortable there than at other theatres. But she had an experience a few years ago that shook that. She was watching a play with a friend, also a black woman, and they were waiting at the bar to get a drink. "This group of white people, I think maybe husband and wife, just went in front of us. I looked at my friend and was like, did you see that? And she just nodded, but eventually I realised they just didn't see us. They didn't think we were there to do something important or watch a show. They thought we were kind of just loitering," she tells me. "I think that was the first experience I had in this theatre where I realised – not because of the theatre, necessarily – but there's an audience that thinks this space belongs to them more than other people."

In the post-pandemic era, Lee-Jones thinks the theatre world will only bring in new audiences if it's really committed to doing so. "They have to keep programming the plays until people feel safe enough to come to the work. And what happened to me in the bar downstairs doesn't keep happening, because people realise: oh, this space is for everyone, it's not just for us." As she's telling me this, just behind her is the Royal Court's building; on the front of it, her name is written in neon lights. How thrilling that, right now, that one belongs to her. [...]

3

Pair work State what you know about Kylie Jenner, the American media celebrity. Find out on the Internet and then decide whether the statements are true or false (if it is false, correct the statement).

	true	false	correction
1. Kylie Jenner is the daughter of Caitlyn and Kris Jenner.			
2. Kylie Jenner belongs to the generation alpha.			
3. She was part of the reality TV series "Keeping up with the Kardashians" because she was adopted by Robert Kardashian.			
4. Jenner launched her own cosmetics line called *Kylie's BW lip kit.*			
5. In 2017, Jenner was placed on the Forbes Celebrity 100 list, making her the youngest person to be featured on the list.			
6. Kylie Jenner beat Mark Zuckerberg by two years when being announced the youngest self-made billionaire in 2019.			
7. Kylie Jenner is black.			

Language

4

a) Users of social media normally don't use formal language. What abbreviations do you use?

CHOOSE

Pair work If you prefer the analogue world you may write the abbreviations down.

OR

Group work You may use the online tool on oncoo.de for this task.

b) Rewrite the following comment in Standard English.

INCOGNEGRO @INCOGNEGRO
Errybody and they aunty need to quit fronting like Kylie killing it! She ain't killing shit! And tbh if I had it my way the only thing geetting kilt would be that bitch! #kyliegjennerfidead (p. 5)

5

Reading social media content in another language can be confusing. All the slang, idioms and abbreviations people use can make even simple sentences tricky to understand.

a) Get acquainted with the abbreviations the protagonists are using by finding the correct partners: which abbreviation means what? Write the matching partners from the box into the table.

actually | Big man thing / honestly in all seriousness | Don't piss me off! | Go on! | I don't care! | Kiss my teeth! | Never mind! | Not gonna lie. | Oh my days! | Say no more! | Swear to god! | to be honest | What are you doing? | What the hell!

abbreviation	meaning
LEWL	*similar to LOL*
DPMO	
OMDS	
BMT	
IDC	
SNM	
S2g	
Nvm	
wyd	
KMT	
ngl	
acc	
WTH	
tbh	
gwarn	

b) Now compare your entries with the list of the most important abbreviations used in the play. You can find a link to the list here: **Webcode** **DSW-73654-04**

c) While reading the play add more abbreviations to the list that are used by the protagonists.

d) Rewrite the following e-mail as a tweet by using as many abbreviations as possible.

> Hello my best friend in the twitter world!
> How are you today? I can't believe we're finally meeting each other. Have I told you that my mom believes you don't exist? That's extremely funny!!!!! However, I can't wait to meet you in real life. I'll see you in Berlin next week!
> Bye for now,
> your dearest friend.

e) CHALLENGE You may add content to make the tweet more realistic.

f) OPTIONAL Rewrite the following hypothetical tweet into Standard English.

> Look @ her DP. What a QT! tbh, that's only in TL – never IRL! Check YT 4 more lies!

WHILE READING

Keeping notes

6

Tip Keeping a reading journal with the focus of summarizing the content as well as adding information about place and time and the relevant page numbers can be one option for remembering the content of a play. Taking notes with a specific focus (e.g. on one of the characters, topics, langauge etc.) is another option to structure the content of a play.

CHOOSE

Focus on one character's perspective: What aspects of Kylie's life are making Cleo furious? Take notes while reading.

OR

Focus on language: The playwright uses words from the black community, like "kiking" (p. 14) "bredrin" (p. 8) etc. Find more examples and explain their meanings.

OR

Focus on language: The play deals with serious topics but in a comical tone. Find examples from the text and evaluate the author's decision to make use of comic elements. Finally fill in your results in the following table:

quotation	topic	effect
1.		
2.		
3.		
4.		

THE PREMEDIATION (PP. 1-3)

7

a) Fill in the table.

1. **Who** are the characters?	
2. **When** do the scenes take place?	
3. **Where** does the action take place?	
4. **What** action is described?	
5. **What** references are made to the world outside the stage?	

b) In the newest version of her play from 2021, Jasmine Lee-Jones makes considerable changes to the PREMEDIATION from the original version from 2019 (see below). If you were Jasmin Lee-Jones and were asked by journalists why you made those changes to the play, apart from "A work of art is never finished" what would you answer?

The present.
In the most present sense of the present tense.
5th March 2019.
Early morning. Outside. A park. Dark.

KARA and CLEO drag something resembling a body onto the platform. They open the traps and throw it in. Cover it with earth. Suddenly they stop, standing over the body.

Blackout.

PART 1 (PP. 4-9): THE START

8

a) Cleo retweets a tweet by Forbes. Describe the "Forbes-tweet" in your own words.

____

b) Cleo is angry about the tweet's hypocrisy. Explain why.

____

c) Cleo creates the hashtag #kyliejennerfidead as a response to the Forbes tweet and tweets hypothetical death threat at Kylie Jenner. Describe Cleo's methods in your own words.

Method # 1: ______________________________

Method # 2: ______________________________

d) Complete the sentence: With tweeting the first two methods of killing, Cleo wants to point out / criticize / make aware of the facts / aim at ...

____

e) Fill in the summary with the appropriate adjectives from the box:

angry | crazy | happy | hypothetical | ingenious | real | surprise | worried

The first part of the plot describes developments in the Twitter world as well as in real life. When the action takes place in ______________ life, Cleo gets a ______________ visit from Kara. Kara had seen Cleo's tweets and wants to know why she is ______________. Cleo plays down the seriousness of her ______________ death threats and therefore wants to calm her ______________ friend.

PART 2 (PP. 10-27): TL AND IRL

9

Social media users are responding to Cleo's tweets (pp. 10-13).

Pair work

a) List the words they are using.

b) Read the infobox. Describe the tweets' tone.

Language support

Talking about the tone

accusatory | admiring | aggressive | ambivalent | amused | appreciative | colloquial | concerned | critical | defensive | dis-/respectful | dis-/approving | judgmental ...

Info

Tone

Tone refers to an author's use of words and writing style to convey his or her attitude towards a topic. Tone is transported through diction (choice of words), viewpoint, syntax (grammar, how you put words together) and level of formality.

c) Explain the following quote in the play's context:

"Inside that tweet is hundreds of years of anti-blackness, positive affirmations of capitalism, cultural appropriation [...]" (p. 15)

d) Name and describe Method # 3 in your own words.

e) Describe the tone of the responses to Method # 3.

f) CHOOSE

Pair work Kara and Cleo are not of the same opinion on various matters. They are having an argument about the tweets' importance (p. 15). List their arguments.

topic of discussion: "It's (just) a tweet"	
Kara	Cleo

OR
Kara and Cleo are having an argument about the application of violence as an answer to oppression (p. 21). List their arguments.

topic of discussion: "violence is the answer to oppression"	
Kara	**Cleo**

g) Cleo has broken up with her boyfriend. Explain why his new girlfriend upsets Cleo.

h) OPTIONAL
Pair work Act out the scene in which the two girls talk about Cleo's boyfriend, the breakup and the new girlfriend.
OR
Group work (4) Create a freeze frame in which the relationships between the following characters become apparent: Cleo, Cleo's boyfriend, the new girlfriend and Kara. You may also add up to three sentences that each character is saying.

The protagonists

10 CHOOSE

Group work What do you get to know about Cleo when reading the play? Write down her profile. Note down the pages, e.g. university student (p. 9).

Age: ______________________________

Education: ______________________________

Family and friends: ______________________________

Topics of interest: ______________________________

Political views: ______________________________

Sexual orientation: ______________________________

Black identity (appearance, language etc.): ______________________________

Character traits: ______________________________

OR
Group work What do you get to know about Kara when reading the play? Write down her profile. Note down the pages.

Age: ______________________________

Education: ______________________________

Family and friends: ______________________________

Topics of interest: ______________________________

Political views: ______________________________

Sexual orientation: ______________________________

Black identity (appearance, language etc.): ______________________________

Character traits: ______________________________

PART 3 (PP. 28-53): BACKGROUND

11

a) Name and describe Method # 4 in your own words.

____

b) Describe the tone of the twitter responses to Method # 4.

____

LISTENING

12

Dr. Kathomi Gatwiri, a senior Academic, psychotherapist and the founder of Healing Together Psychotherapy is talking about the term "gaslighting". You can find a link to the video here: **Webcode** **DSW-73654-05**

a) Listen to the first part of episode 1: "Racial gaslighting" (00:00-3:28). Decide whether the following sentences are right or wrong. Correct the statements when they are wrong.

	right	wrong	correction
1. Gaslighting is a form of physical abuse.			
2. People who are being gaslighted know that they are being manipulated and are therefore content about their knowledge.			
3. The term refers to a movie in which a husband convinces his wife that she is just imagining the dimming of lights.			
4. Racial gaslighting is when people of colour are told that their experiences are acknowledged.			
5. Racial gaslighting is deliberately used to maintain white supremacy.			
6. The more black people resist to this racial hierarchy the more acceptance they are experiencing in society.			

b) "My own bredrin gaslighting me" (p. 32). Explain Cleo's accusation.

13

Which sentences about Kara's and Cleo's past are correct? Give proof from the text. → **S23:** How to quote

- The primary school teachers admired Cleo's curly hair.
- Cleo was always in Kara's shadow.
- Cleo had many boyfriends when she was young.
- Kara is satisfied with her appearance.
- Cleo accuses Kara of not having helped her at a party.

14

a) Name and describe Method # 5.

____

b) Describe the tweets responding to Cleo's method # 5. What historical references are made? (twitterludes 4 and 5)

____

PART 4 (PP. 54-78): CHANGES

15

a) Cleo's tweets get out of hand when one of her older tweets is re-tweeted by someone else.

- What gets re-tweeted and why?

____

- How does Cleo respond?

____

b) **Pair work** Both Cleo and Kara share stories from the past to explain when they felt misunderstood by each other.

- Partner A: Outline Cleo's story of #wiggate (pp. 45-48).
- Partner B: Outline Kara's story of T'Sharn's 13th birthday party (p. 66).
- Give feedback on how well the summary was performed by your partner.

c) CHALLENGE

Comment on the following statement: "If they had acted differently in the past their relationship now would be a different one". Justify your answer.

d) Name and describe Method #6.

____

e) Put these events into the right order:

☐ Her identity in real life is revealed on Twitter.
☐ Cleo's IRL and TL identities merge into one.
☐ Cleo and Kara have a fight about Cleo's behaviour at T'sham's birthday party.
☐ Cleo is blocked from following Kara's Twitter account.
☐ Someone on TL re-tweets a comment by Cleo accusing her of being homophobic.
☐ Cleo apologizes for the two homophobic tweets from 2014.

f) In Method # 7, Cleo wants Kylie Jenner to experience the same mistreatments that Saartjie must have gone through. Which mistreatments does Cleo mean? Describe the historical context Cleo is referring to.

PART 5 (PP. 79-83): THE END

16

a) With the sentence "I just don't wanna feel heavy no more" (p. 79) Cleo describes a burden she is carrying. From what burden does Cleo need to be freed?

b) Saartjie's spirit is appearing. What are Kara and Cleo praising her for?

c) The image from the PREMEDIATION of Cleo and Kara standing over a body reappears in the POST-MORTEM.

> **Info**
> The post mortem interval is the time that has elapsed since a person has died. The term can also be applied to the post mortem examination of a corpse in order to determine the cause of death.

Why do you think Jasmine Lee-Jones chose this title for the last scene?

POST-READING

Relationships

17

a) Describe the friendship between Kara and Cleo.

> **Help** Look at the following pages: 7-9, 21-25, 32-40, 48-49, 59-60, 66, 69-73, 79ff.
> Then draw a table like the one below.

section	content	description of their friendship / relationship

b) In the following quote Cleo makes a reference to slaverey on a plantation:
"Back in the old days I'd be the field nigger out shucking corn and you'd be in the house beating the master." (p. 39)
- Explain the parallels she is drawing.
- What does the quote reveal about the friendship between Cleo and Kara?

c) Kara is blocking Cleo from following @KARA and viewing her tweets. Describe Cleo's reaction. How would you feel if your best friend did that to you?

d) **Pair work** At the end of the play, Cleo and Kara share a spiritual encounter with Snaartjie.
- Does this experience strengthen their friendship?
- Discuss: Will they stay friends?

18 CHOOSE

Group work Create five freeze frames in which you show the development of Kara and Cleo's relationship. You may act between the freeze frames.

OR

Choose a part of Cleo and Kara's conversation described on the pages 32 to 35, l. 3. Act out the scene.

19

Pair work Talk for five minutes about the question in the bubble and come to a conclusion.

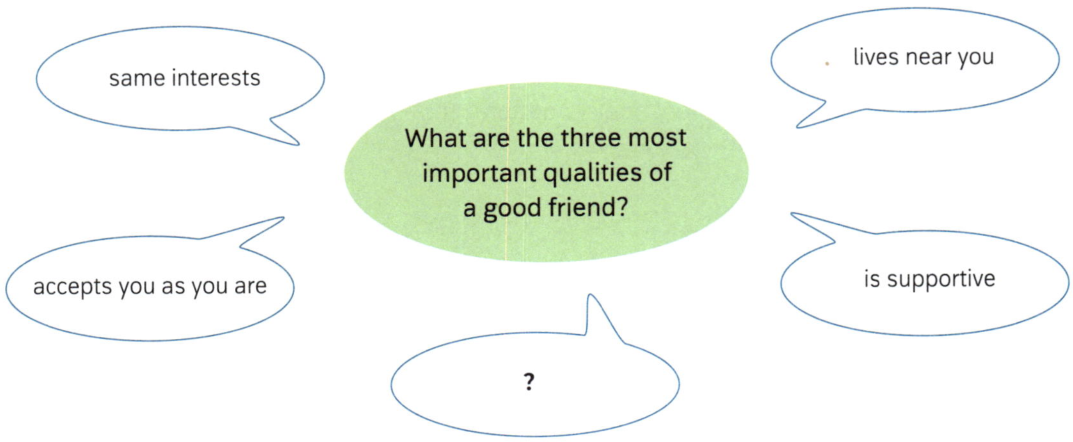

Characterization

20 CHOOSE

Write a characterization of Cleo (including her online and offline identity)

OR

Kara.

Consider if Cleo's and / or Kara's character develop throughout the play. Illustrate and proove it with the text.

> Tip You can find language support for writing a characterization in *Camden Town Oberstufe* on page 353.

→ **Workshop:** Analysing characters → **S23:** How to quote

Illustrations and graphic layout of the play's script

21

a) On social media, words are often flanked by photos, emojis, cartoons etc. Look at the following pages: 4, 10, 12, 13, 17, 44.

b) Explain the combined use of language and illustrations in TL. Draw a box like the one below and fill in your findings.
- Define the type of illustration. Is it a photo, a film still, an emoji, a gif, a meme, a cartoon etc?
- What are the illustrations showing?
- How are illustrations used to transport meaning?

	type of illustration (photo, gif, emoji, cartoon, film still ...)?	What does it show?	Why is it used? What is the meaning?
1. p. 4			

c) Find more examples and add them to the list.

d) CHALLENGE Describe the layout of words and the way some words are written. What could be the reason people use such a layout?

e) CHALLENGE There are parts in the play where the TL seems to intersect with the IRL, e.g. pictures are shown IRL (pp. 22, 34, 45, 71-73). What could be the playwright's intention?

Putting the play on stage

22

The director of a play decides how elements of the play script can be transferred to the stage.

a) **Group work** Come up with an option for how TL can be staged. Consider how light, sound, actors, stage and audience can play a role.

b) Watch the video of a scene from a production and note down how TL is staged. Explain the effect on the audience. You can find a link to the video here: **Webcode** **DSW-73654-06**

c) Take a look at the production photos from the version staged at the Royal Court Theatre in London in 2021. Considering the elements on stage (cables, purple-blue cloud, dark background) and the actors' gestures, what part of the play could be shown? You can find a link to the photo gallery here: **Webcode** **DSW-73654-07**

VIPs

23

Cleo and Kara are making references to various famous people existing in IRL.

Joanne The Scammer | Cardi B | Angela Davis | Maxine Water | MLK | Saartjie (Sarah Baartman)

a) **Group work** Placemat: Get into groups using the placemat method:
- Each member finds out about one historical figure.
- Write your findings into your section of the placemat.
- Turn the placemat clockwise so that you can read your teammates' findings.
- Discuss and agree on a result, which you write into the group section in the middle.
- Present your results in front of the class.

b) Discuss: To what extent are these people important for the context of the play?

Body images

24

a) CHOOSE Choose a country: Iran, Japan, New Zealand, Brazil, France, Kenya, South Korea, Mauritania, Oman or United States and prepare a two minute talk on the beauty standard of this country as it is described in the video "How Beauty standards differ around the world". You can find a link to the video here: **Webcode** **DSW-73654-08**

Info

Body image

Body image refers to a person's emotional attitudes, beliefs, and perceptions of their own body. [...]
Body image relates to
- what a person believes about their appearance
- how they feel about their body, height, weight, and shape
- how they sense and control their body as they move

A person's body image will range from positive, or satisfaction with their body, to negative, or dissatisfaction with their body.

b) Who defines what beauty is? Explain the following quote in the context of body image as it is described in the info box:
"[...] and even Miss Fitzgerald always said how pretty your hair was, and the only time she came remotely close to commenting on how nice my hair was, was when my Mum straightened it for the Year 5 pictures." (p. 35)

25 Pair work

Now take a look at the following photo by Carrie Mae Weems of a woman in front of a mirror. You can find a link here: **Webcode** DSW-73654-09. What does she want to show the viewer about black body image / ethnic identity? Explain.

a) Read the quote by Jasmine Lee-Jones.

> I keep a scrapbook with pictures for everything that I write. The main image is currently [art by Carrie Mae Weems] of a black woman looking in the mirror saying "Mirror, mirror on the wall, who's the fairest of them all?" and the mirror's response is "Snow White, you black bitch." That's very much this play.

Elements and structure of a play

26

a) Label the following elements of a play script: stage directions, scene, characters, title, setting, playwright, text and cast.

Seven methods of killing Kylie Jenner ← 1. ____________

by Jasmine Lee-Jones ← 2. ____________

← 3. ____________

Cleo a.k.a @INCOGNEGRO
Kara

Leanne Henlon
Tia Bannon ← 4. ____________

1. ← 5. ____________

5th March 2019 4:01 AM ← 6. ____________
The bird expands and suddenly we are on Twitter.

.... ← 7. ____________

Suddenly a figure enters lurking. She creeps on CLEO; touches her.
[...]

KARA: (*in a roadman lilt.*) Fuck are you on blad! ← 8. ____________

b) Normally, the development of the plot follows a certain structure as shown below.

- Does the play meet this scheme?
- Where can you see contemporary elements?

> Tip: You can find an explanation of the different terms in *Camden Town Oberstufe* on page 350.

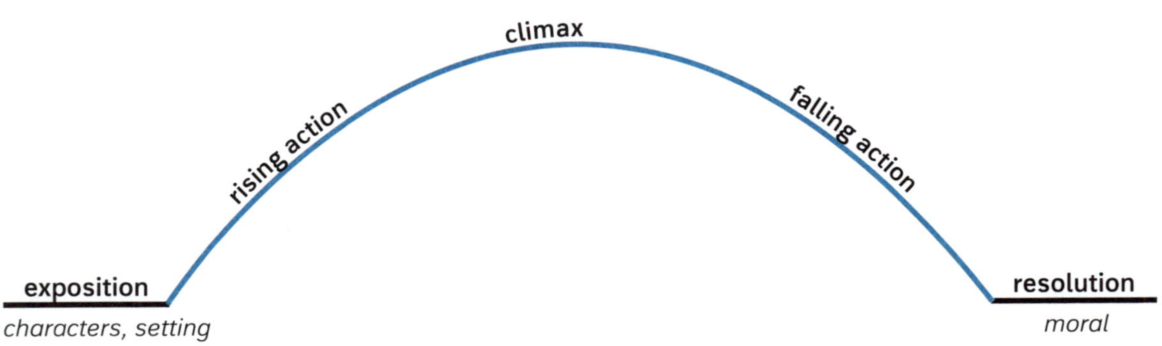

Reviews

27

a) Lee-Jones created a contemporary theatre play that has been widely reviewed. Compare the two opinions by Kate Wywer (1.) and Natasher Beecher (2.).

1. Although the physicalisation of the internet is imaginative, the Twitter-interlude structure feels a little trapped towards the end, as if it's stopped inventing. The arguments begin to circle and the finale can't quite hold the weight of history it attempts to. Nevertheless, Henlon and Bannon are gripping throughout. Jones is a brilliant, dynamic writer, and this is a striking debut.

2. For us black women '*Seven methods of killing kylie Jenner*' with its blend of nostalgia and heart, is us being seen and being heard in a way that's almost too difficult to watch, our collective trauma laid bare. [...]

   For anyone who isn't black, and white people, in particular, this play will resonate with you in a magical way that you won't quite understand. But one thing is for sure, this poignant play that goes beyond just the zeitgeist is for everyone. It's a play for now and for after – a cultural marker of the way the world is changing and needs to change. Everyone should go see it.

b) CHOOSE

Write a review as a tweet.

OR

Write a review for a broadsheet newspaper.

The influence of social media on young people's identity

1

a) **Pair work** Brainstorming: list advantages and disadvantages of using social media.

b) Explain the chart. → **S18:** How to analyse statistics

Mental Health: The Impact of Social Media on Young People

Ranking of social media platforms according to impact on youth mental health

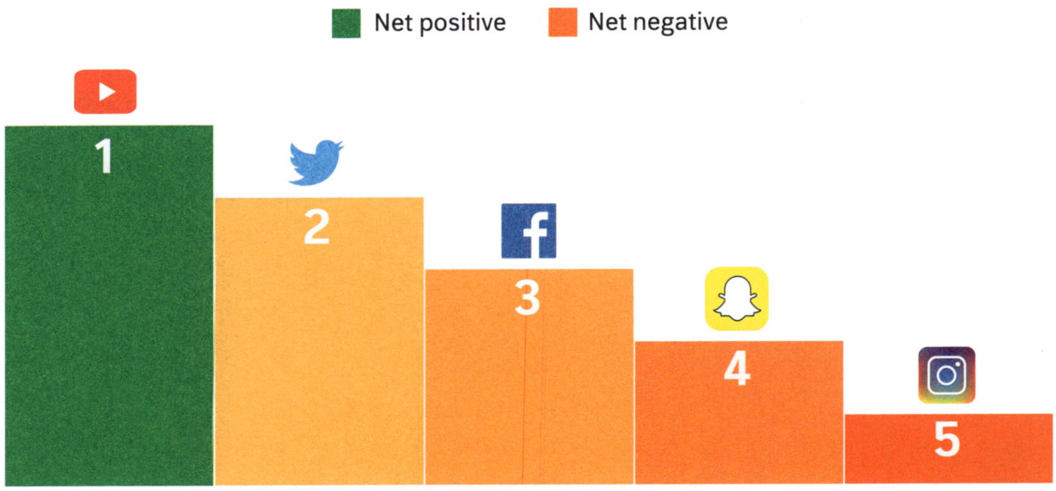

Survey conducted in the United Kingdom among 1,479 young people between the ages of 14 and 24. 14 factors were taken into account such as anxiety, depression, loneliness, self-image, harassment, opportunity to express oneself.

Source: Statista; 2019

c) **Pair work** Discuss: Would you take part in a school challenge of a social media free week?

2

Tweets play a major role in *seven methods of killing kylie jenner* and are responsible for the play's development.

a) Examine to what extent the twitter comments are changing in the course of the play. Fill in the table with keywords.

content twitterludes	Who is writing?	scale of factual information (1 true to 9 false)	scale of humour (1 little to 9 the most)	scale of hatred (1 little to 9 the most)
1				
2				

content twitterludes	Who is writing?	scale of factual information (1 true to 9 false)	scale of humour (1 little to 9 the most)	scale of hatred (1 little to 9 the most)
3				
4				
5				
6				
7				
8				
9				
10				
11				

b) Choose from the following adjectives to describe the development: use a timeline / graph / colour scheme to illustrate.

accusing | amused | conspirational | funny | homophobic | inflammatory | international | irritated | misogynist | racist | sexist | shocked | surprised

c) With the increasing usage of digital technologies, a new form of bullying has emerged: "cyberbullying". Have you or your friends ever experienced cyberbullying? Illustrate (topics, feelings, consequences).

d) **Pair work** At what point in the development of the twitterludes do you think cyberbullying starts? Give reasons.

3

Cleo and Kara are having a discussion about the reactions to the death threats against Cleo that are announced in TL (pp. 43-44).

a) List their arguments. Give your opinion.

b) Cleo describes the following humiliating incident. What is happening?

"Cameras flashing without my consent
Over and over
Images posted all over socials
Me a meme
A silent, unconsenting gif
Like I was some sort of spectacle
Or a fucking freak
I've never felt so ugly in my life." (p. 48)

c) Taking photos – now and fifty years ago: what has changed? What role does social media play today compared to then?

d) Internet research: Find out about the rules of taking photographs in public and private areas in Germany.

The role of ethnic identity on (social) media

4

a) Cleo is a black woman having an identity in real life and in twitter life ("incognegro") and for both identities, her ethnic identity seems to play a role. How are these identities connected?

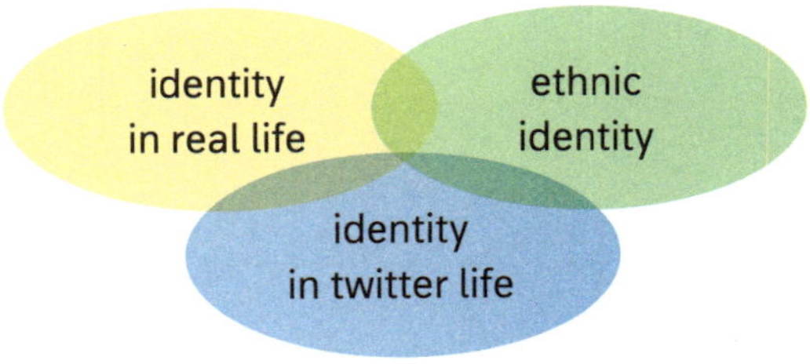

b) CHOOSE Take one of the quotes concerning the topic "skin colour" and explain it in the context of the conversation between Cleo and Kara.

- "You don't own blackness just because you're dark-skinned!" (p. 37)

OR

- "You are a lightie" (p. 33)

OR

- "All the BW considered universally beautiful are lighties" (p. 34)

Stating your opinion

5 → **S6:** How to write a discussion / comment → **S9:** How to structure a text → **S8:** How to improve your text

Cleo shows her anger by creating hypothetical death threats to Kylie Jenner.

a) CHOOSE

Write a comment on the question of whether you think social media is a good channel to state your opinion.

OR

Pair work Write an electronic text together with a partner in a collaborative document.

> **Help** Alternative options to state your opinion and make it public:
> - going on a strike
> - talking to people face-to-face
> - sending emails or letters to the government
> - starting a petition

b) Why did the playwright choose to include twitter in her play?

MEDIATION

6 → **S19:** How to improve your mediation skills

a) Read the article.

b) Write an email to the playwright Jasmine Lee-Jones in which you describe the latest development in Germany concerning the influence of social media on politics. Refer to her play by pointing out parallels.

Anfeindungen gegen Sarah-Lee Heinrich
Medienexpertin: Koordinierte Twitter-Kampagnen als Methode

Immer häufiger werden Akteure aus Politik und Medien im Netz mit fragwürdigen Aussagen aus ihrer Vergangenheit konfrontiert. Dabei gerate aus dem Blick, aus welchen Kreisen diese Enthüllungen stammen, sagte Tajana Graovac vom „No Hate Speech Movement" im Dlf.

The German politician Sarah-Lee Heinrich

Ein paar Tweets können reichen, damit bei Twitter und darüber hinaus innerhalb weniger Stunden eine große Debatte in Gang kommt. So war das zuletzt zum Beispiel im Fall der neuen Bundessprecherin der Grünen Jugend.

Sarah-Lee Heinrich geriet in den Fokus wegen mehrerer alter Nachrichten, in denen sie im Jahr 2015 zum Beispiel „Heil" unter einen Tweet mit Hakenkreuz geschrieben hatte. Die heute 20-Jährige schrieb, sie könne sich nicht daran erinnern, als Jugendliche jemals einen solchen Tweet abgesetzt zu haben.„Das war maximal dumm und unangebracht", schrieb Heinrich. Die Sozialwissenschafts-Studentin betonte aber auch, dass sie sich „jetzt nicht zu allem erklären" wolle, „was ich mal so mit 14 gedacht und gesagt habe".

Erst Tweets, dann Morddrohungen

Heinrich beklagte außerdem, seit ihrer Wahl versuchten Rechte, Shitstorms gegen sie hochzuziehen: „Haben wohl Bammel vor einer schwarzen, linken Frau", schrieb Heinrich. Nach diesen Tweets zog sich Heinrich vorerst aus der Öffentlichkeit zurück. Der Grünen-Jugendorganisation zufolge hatte sie Mord- und Gewaltandrohungen erhalten. Es gehe „jetzt erst einmal darum, alles für ihre Sicherheit zu tun", sagte der scheidende Bundessprecher der Grünen Jugend, Georg Kurz.

„Das ist koordiniert"

Dass der Fall eine solche Entwicklung genommen hat, sei typisch, sagte Tajana Graovac vom „No Hate Speech Movement" im Deutschlandfunk „Was wir feststellen können, dass es große Accounts sind, die meistens eher in der rechten Ecke zu finden sind, die große Reichweite haben", sagte Graovac.

Accounts aus rechten und rechtsextremen Kreisen würden dann dafür sorgen, dass sich die entsprechenden Nachrichten weit verbreiten. „Das ist koordiniert. Und es ist tatsächlich auch immer das gleiche Schema und das geht fast immer nach der gleichen Dynamik", so Graovac weiter.

Manipulierte Kampagnen erkennen

Zudem würden zum Teil Screenshots verbreitet, die nachträglich manipuliert worden seien. „Man schneidet die Zeit und das Datum ab, damit die irgendwie auch aktuell aussehen. Es werden teilweise Wörter weggelassen, damit die Tweets noch schlimmer klingen. Und das zieht dann wirklich Kreise.“ Aufgabe von Journalistinnen und Journalisten sei es, dies zu erkennen und nicht auf eine Kampagne hereinzufallen. Sie müssten offenlegen, „dass es eine gezielte, koordinierte Attacke ist gegen eine schwarze Person“.

Cartoon analysis – images of black female identity

7 → **S17:** How to work with cartoons

a) Study the woman's depiction in the cartoon carefully, then describe it.

b) Explain the cartoon's message by referring to its individual elements.

c) Come up with a possible title and give reasons for your decision.

Language support

index finger | megaphone | speech bubble

d) Black women are regularly depicted in the media and society as 'angry', 'aggressive' and 'sassy'. Imagine in which situations black women could be seen as behaving in an "angry" way?

e) Read the following Wikipedia entry on this stereotype. You can find a link to the text here:
Webcode **DSW-73654-10**

Pair work

- Sum up the text in keywords and compare your result with a partner.

f) Discuss how it is possible for black women to escape the vicious circle of being referred to as an "angry black woman" when they show anger about being called this term.
You may refer to M. Obama's reactions described in the following newspaper excerpt:

Michelle Obama: 'I'm no angry black woman'

The Obamas, by New York Times reporter Jodi Kantor, portrays her as a behind-the-scenes force in the White House.

[...] Mrs Obama did not deny being an important voice to her husband.

"I am his biggest ally," Mrs Obama said. "I am one of his biggest confidants. But he has dozens of really smart people who surround him. That's not to say that we don't have discussions and conversations."

"I guess it's more interesting to imagine this conflicted situation here and a strong woman. But that's been an image that people have tried to paint of me since the day Barack announced [he would run for president] – that I'm some angry black woman," she said.

"I just try to be me. And my hope is that over time people get to know me," she told CBS. "And they get to judge me for me." [...]

8

a) Read the article.

b) Outline Ritu Prasad's view on the myth of the "angry black woman" as presented in this article.

___

___

___

Serena Williams and the trope[1] of the 'angry black woman'

by Ritu Prasad

Mammies, jezebels, Sapphires. Black women in America have long been dogged by negative stereotypes, rooted in a history of racism and slavery. In the aftermath of Serena Williams' controversial US Open loss, it's the trope of the "angry black woman" that has once again re-emerged.

During the US Open final, Williams received a code violation for coaching[2], a penalty point for breaking her racquet and a game penalty for calling the umpire a "thief". And later, a fine of $17,000 (£13,000).

Her reactions to the referee's calls – which the Women's Tennis Association has since decri[b]ed as "sexist" – were no different from how many top players react in the heat of a championship game.

But it was the way she was punished for her anger that has sparked further outrage.

[...] The law professor and tennis fan Prof Trina Jones has studied racial stereotyping and how it plays into the lives of African-American women.

"Black women are not supposed to push back and when they do, they're deemed to be domineering. Aggressive. Threatening. Loud." Similar words have been levelled at[3] Serena Williams more than once, as well as former First Lady Michelle Obama and top Democrat Maxine Waters in recent years.

Prof Jones says some have compared the referee's calls to speeding tickets: many people speed and sometimes a few are caught. But that analogy, she says, misses the point that African Americans are disproportionately pulled aside. In the case of Williams, she was first dinged[4] on a coaching violation that happens often but is rarely called out as the player's fault. "Why would a black woman in a championship match therefore be called on it?" Prof Jones says, adding that an attack on one's integrity is only natural to be angry about. "[Williams] is outraged because she knows the context."

The myth of the 'angry black woman'

The "angry black woman" trope has its roots in 19th Century America, when minstrel shows, which

Annotations

[1] **trope** = *Tropus, bildlicher Ausdruck*

[2] **coaching** = Players aren't allowed to be coached in Grand Slam matches. Violations lead to warnings or penalties.

[3] to **be levelled at** = thrown at / labels given to her without much consideration or thought

[4] to **be dinged** = sharp riging sound; here: held to account

Annotations
[5] **comic skit** = a comedy sketch
[6] **sassy** = *frech*
[7] **pervasive** = common
[8] to **grapple** = to fight with or to continually discuss a difficult issue
[9] **clarion call** = appeal

involved comic skits[5] and variety acts, mocking African Americans became popular. Blair Kelley, associate professor of history at North Carolina State University, says black women were often played by overweight white men who painted their faces black and donned fat suits "to make them look less than human, unfeminine, ugly". "Their main way of interacting with the men around them was to scream and fight and come off angry, irrationally so, in response to the circumstances around them," she says. "The real problem in their everyday life was not the structural things that black people faced, but the mouth of the black woman – her tone, her irrationality and her anger," Prof Kelley says of Sapphire's role.

As segregation laws known as Jim Crow laws saw black Americans assaulted, jailed and killed, popular culture pushed ideas of "sassy[6] mammies" and "Sapphires" – an archetype depicting black women with iron-fists, yelling at everyone from children to white men. [...] This trope of the "angry black woman" has endured, and has been pervasive[7] in modern media even without more overtly racist portrayals, says Brandi Collins, senior campaign director at the racial justice organisation Color of Change.

On screen, it is easy to push sass for laughs. But black women in America see these depictions translate differently in real life. For Ms Collins, the picture of the "hyperemotional" black woman has become more commonplace as Americans grapple[8] with issues of polarised politics and civility. Black women, she says, are often faced with people responding to their emotions "from a place of perceived fear. There's almost a paranoia around it. A feeling that you have to go above and beyond to make people feel comfortable around you."

Robin Boylorn, an intercultural communications professor at the University of Alabama told the BBC it seems impossible to be a black woman and not be angry, after "generations of oppression, discrimination and erasure". "Black women should be celebrated for not being completely consumed by anger," she says.

"Men are allowed to be angry as a performance of masculinity. White women are allowed to be angry as a clarion call[9]. So black women should be encouraged to express their anger as well, particularly in the face of injustice."

[...] Ms Collins notes that fixing the problem is not just about eliminating the "angry black woman" trope. "For every type of white man you can imagine, there's a movie about his story and his experience and his journey. Black women in media aren't afforded that diversity of experience," she says. Instead, understanding the diversity of a black woman's experience – and not just her anger – is the key.

For Williams, that's a lesson she hopes her fans will learn from her US Open upset. "I'm here to fight for women's rights and women's equality. The fact that I have to go through this is an example," she told reporters after the match. "Maybe it didn't work out for me, but it's going to work out for the next person."

9

Explain why it is inadequate to refer to an African American woman as an "angry black woman".

Looking back at the play

10

Pair work Cleo is being criticized for her behaviour in the TL, e.g. "I for one can't believe @INCOGNEGRO acting like dis. U ain't the next civil rights activist." (p. 19).

Are there any more parallels between Serena Williams' depiction as an angry woman and the comments in TL that describe Cleo as hysterical and over-reacting?

11

Group work Your school is planning a project week with the topic "school for the future" and is asking students to send in podcasts, videos, posters, etc. with ideas of how schools can address and eliminate racism. What would be your contribution?

Pre-reading

1

Hamlet is one of William Shakespeare's later tragedies, written around 1600-1602. It is set at the Danish royal court.
To get some ideas about the setting and atmosphere of the play, carefully study the photos below. Then choose the adjectives or expressions from the box that best describe the atmosphere the photos convey. Give reasons.

cold | spooky | vast | remote | fortified | belligerent | grand | on the brink of war | gloomy | depressing | wintry

2

As you have gained some insight into the setting, find out about the characters in *Hamlet*.

a) Read the short descriptions of the characters below and on page 122. Then start a character map in which you show the relationships between them. Add additional information to your map while you read the play.

Hamlet
the son of the late king Hamlet and the nephew of the present king; a student at the University of Wittenberg

Claudius
King of Denmark and brother of the former king. He has killed his brother.

Gertrude
Queen of Denmark, Claudius' wife and Hamlet's mother; after the death of her first husband, the former king, she recently married his brother

Polonius
Claudius' counsellor, father of Ophelia and Laertes

Ophelia
Hamlet's true love, Polonius' daughter. She drowns later on in the play.

Laertes
Polonius' son and Ophelia's brother, a student in France

Horatio
Hamlet's best friend and fellow student at Wittenberg University

Fortinbras
the young Prince of Norway, whose father (also called Fortinbras) was killed by Hamlet's father (also called Hamlet)

The Ghost
An other-worldly presence who has taken on the form of old King Hamlet. He tells Hamlet that his father was murdered by Claudius and he should avenge him.

Rosencrantz and Guildenstern
two of Hamlet's former friends from Wittenberg, summoned by Claudius and Gertrude to find out about the reasons for Hamlet's melancholy

Voltemand and Cornelius
Danish ambassadors who are sent to Norway to negotiate peace

Marcellus and Bernardo
Danish military officers and casual friends of Hamlet who first see the ghost walking the ramparts of Elsinore Castle

Francisco
a soldier and guardsman

Reynaldo
Polonius' servant who is sent to France by his master to spy on Laertes

Players
a group of actors who come to Elsinore to perform a play partially written by Hamlet

Osric
a foolish courtier who, on Claudius' order, summons Hamlet to take part in a duel with Laertes

Two clowns
gravediggers who discuss various issues while digging a grave

b) Having caught a first glimpse at the characters involved, outline what you expect from the play.

Language support

I expect the play to be full of intrigue/corruption/revenge/...
I think that ... will try to plot against .../avenge .../commit murder/...
From what I have read, I assume the play will be fast-paced/action-packed/a romance/...

3

There is no evidence to be found in Shakespeare's biography that he ever visited Denmark. So where did he get his idea of a Danish prince avenging his father's death from?

a) Watch an extract from a video and tick the correct answers. Before watching the extract (00:00-02:00), read the questions carefully. **Webcode** DSW-73654-11

1 Where does the recording take place?
- ❑ in Denmark
- ❑ in a London loft
- ❑ at the Danish Embassy in London

2 Why did Shakespeare choose Kronborg Castle for the setting of Elsinore in *Hamlet*?
- ❑ He liked the castle very much.
- ❑ There are a lot of explanations for it.
- ❑ He read about it.

3 When did a troupe of English actors come to Kronborg Castle?
❑ in 1518
❑ in 1568
❑ in 1586

4 How do people know about this visit?
❑ There are records of the payment the actors received.
❑ Shakespeare mentions it in his work.
❑ It was commonly known in London at the time.

5 Where did the theatre players come from?
❑ London
❑ Leicester
❑ Copenhagen

6 What was the name of the actors' troupe?
❑ The King's Group
❑ London Group
❑ Leicester Group

7 What was special about Kronborg Castle?
❑ It was the biggest Renaissance castle in northern Europe.
❑ It had the highest tower in Denmark.
❑ It was the Danish king's main residence.

8 How did Shakespeare know about the castle?
❑ He was one of the three actors visiting the castle.
❑ The three actors told Shakespeare about the place.
❑ Ambassadors told him about the castle.

9 Did Shakespeare really visit the castle?
❑ Yes, he did.
❑ No, he did not.
❑ It is not certain.

b) It is widely believed that Shakespeare was inspired by a version of the Scandinavian legend of *Amleth* by the Danish author Saxo Grammaticus (1150-1220). Research this legend and then show the characters' relationship in the character map below.

Gervendill *Koll*

Horvendill *Feng*

Gerutha *young girl*

Amleth

Rørik Slyngebond *princess of England*

King of England *Wiglek*

Hermuthruda

While reading: Act I

SCENE I: THE OPENING SCENE OF THE PLAY

1

The play opens with a changing of the guard at the royal court of Elsinore Castle in Denmark. Francisco, who is on sentry duty, is relieved by Bernardo. Horatio and Marcellus arrive to join Bernardo. The country is on the brink of war with Norway.

a) Read the first part of the opening scene of the play (ll. 1-107) and try to understand as much as possible. Then answer the following questions:

1. What time is it when Bernardo relieves Francisco? ______

______

2. How does Francisco feel and why? ______

______

3. What was his guard duty like? ______

______

4. What did Marcellus and Bernardo witness on their guard duty the previous two nights? ______

______

5. What does Horatio think about their report at first? ______

______

6. Why has Marcellus asked Horatio to join them on their guard duty? ______

______

7. How does Horatio react when he sees what the soldiers told him about? ______

______

______

b) In the opening scenes of his plays, Shakespeare uses language to attract the audience's attention and to make them curious about what will happen next. Bear in mind that in Elizabethan theatres there were hardly any props or scenery to indicate the setting. All this has to be done through language. Identify the means Shakespeare uses for these different purposes and analyse them.
Use a grid like this one.

lines	*text*	*analysis*
1	*Who's there?*	*question suggests that Bernardo can't see anything → shows it is dark and that Bernardo is nervous*
...	...	...

c) In class, talk about why Shakespeare opens his play in such a manner.

2

Horatio believes his friends now and tells them why Denmark is preparing for war.

a) Read lines 134-174 of the first scene of Act I and retell Horatio's story using the cues in the box below.

> to reach an agreement | sealed contract | to reclaim land | a bunch of outlaws | to wage war against | to die in combat | to lose territories | to stand guard | to prepare for war

b) **Group work (5)** While one student reads the lines slowly, the other members act out the lines.

3

Many plays open with a scene that sows the seeds of a catastrophe that will follow.

a) Speculate what disastrous events may occur during the course of the play.

b) Explain how the first scene foreshadows these events.

4 CHOOSE **Group work (4-5)**

Talk about how you would stage the opening scene.
Consider

- the first thing the audience sees.
- how you bring across the atmosphere and how the short sentences or questions contribute to the overall atmosphere.
- how each character speaks (nervously, clearly, calmly, forcefully, boldly, etc.).
- how you bring the setting across: In Shakespeare's time the play would have been staged at broad daylight. Which words or phrases help to create the impression of night and darkness?
- whether the audience sees the apparition?

Present your ideas to the class.

OR

Hamlet has been turned into a film many times. Here are some examples of the opening scenes:

- battle scenes between Denmark and Norway with old King Hamlet wounded
- old King Hamlet's funeral procession
- flags on the walls of Elsinore Castle signifying the death of old King Hamlet
- the queen crying at the tomb of her husband
- a chef peeping around a curtain to see if the next course can be served at a banquet

Assess the examples listed above. Then devise your own version that accompanies the credits and leads to the first line of text spoken by a character.

SCENE II

5

Claudius, recently crowned King of Denmark, enters the stage, addressing his courtiers.

a) Read his address (ll. 1-43). Then decide whether the statements below are true or false. Correct them if necessary.

	Statement	Evidence	true	false
1	Despite King Hamlet's recent death and the nation's mourning, Claudius needs to consider his own position.			
2	In a very joyful ceremony, Claudius has married his brother's widow.			
3	His courtiers advised him against marrying Gertrude.			
4	Fortinbras holds a poor opinion of Claudius.			
5	Fortinbras seems to think that Denmark is in a chaotic state after King Hamlet's death.			
6	Fortinbras wants to reclaim the lands his father lost to the late Danish king.			
7	Claudius has written a letter, asking the powerful King of Norway to stop his nephew's activities.			
8	Claudius sends two ambassadors to Norway.			

b) **Pair work** Talk about how Claudius comes across. Does he seem devious or honest, resolute or weak?

c) **Pair work** Talk about what words you would particularly stress in the speech. Then read out the King's address.

6

Claudius and Gertrude are worried about Hamlet and talk to him.

a) Read the extract (ll. 79-143). Then match the following statements to the characters Gertrude, Hamlet and Claudius and give the line reference.

Statement	Lines	Character
Your behaviour is a sin against God's will and against nature.		
Stay with us and do not go back to Wittenberg.		
Stop wearing black clothes.		
You are the next in line for the throne.		
Stop mourning for your father's death.		
It is unmanly for a son to grieve so long for a dead father.		
The sighing, the weeping, the downcast eyes – other people may use all this to put on a show.		
It is normal for people to die. So why are you so extremely sad, nonetheless?		
My clothes hint at the real grief I feel.		

b) Analyse the relationship between Hamlet, Gertrude and Claudius.

c) **Group work (3)** Act out the extract. Use emphasis and intonation to convey the characteristics of the relationship between the three characters.

7

After talking to his mother and uncle, Hamlet remains alone on stage. Read his following soliloquy below.

a) Structure the soliloquy and label the different parts. The first one has been done for you.

Text	Annotations	Notes
O, that this too, too solid flesh would melt,	**to thaw** to melt	
Thaw and resolve itself into a dew,	**to resolve** to dissolve	
Or that the Everlasting had not fixed	**the Everlasting** God	*Hamlet contemplates suicide*
His canon 'gainst self-slaughter. O God, God,	**canon** divine law	
How weary, stale, flat and unprofitable	**self-slaughter** suicide **stale** old, tasteless	
Seem to me all the uses of this world!	**uses** business	
Fie on't! ah fie, 'tis an unweeded garden,	**Fie on't** To hell with it.	
That grows to seed, things rank and gross in nature	**unweeded** without the weeds (*Unkraut*) having been removed	
Possess it merely. That it should come to this:		
But two months dead – nay, not so much, not two –	**grows to seed** becomes overgrown with undesirable plants	
So excellent a king, that was, to this		
Hyperion to a satyr, so loving to my mother	**rank** growing without limit	
That he might not beteem the winds of heaven		
Visit her face too roughly. Heaven and earth,	**gross** dense, thick **in nature** as is natural	
Must I remember? Why, she would hang on him	**merely** completely	
As if increase of appetite had grown	**to beteem** (archaic) to allow	
By what it fed on. And yet, within a month	**hang on him** be so in love with him	
(Let me not think on't – Frailty, thy name is Woman),	**on't** about it	
A little month, or ere those shoes were old	**frailty** weakness	
With which she followed my poor father's body,	**ere** before	
Like Niobe, all tears. Why she, even she –		
O God, a beast that wants discourse of reason	**wants discourse of reason** does not have the ability to think	
Would have mourned longer – married with my uncle,		
My father's brother (but no more like my father		
Than I to Hercules). Within a month,		
Ere yet the salt of most unrighteous tears	**unrighteous** insincere	
Had left the flushing in her gallèd eyes,	**flushing** flowing tears	
She married. O most wicked speed, to post	**gallèd** irritated **to post** to hurry	
With such dexterity to incestuous sheets!	**dexterity** haste	
It is not, nor it cannot come to good.		
But break, my heart, for I must hold my tongue.		

b) Sum up what Hamlet criticizes his mother for.

c) Read the info box below. Use the information to discuss the function of this soliloquy.

Info

Soliloquy

Soliloquy is the act of talking to oneself. This can be done silently or aloud. In drama, the term describes the practice by which a character, alone on stage, utters his or her thoughts for the audience to hear. Soliloquies serve as a dramatic device to let the audience know about the character's intentions and state of mind, and also to give additional information about the action of the play.

Soliloquies are often used to

- set the scene
- make the audience part of the play
- explicate the character's feelings
- clarify matters
- introduce further information

SCENE III

8

Laertes is about to go back to Paris. Before he goes, he takes his leave of his sister.

a) Read the dialogue between Ophelia and Laertes (ll. 1-61). Then tick the pieces of advice Laertes really gives Ophelia and give the line reference.

Be aware that Hamlet might only toy with you.	✓	*l.10: "the trifling of his favour"*
Hamlet's feelings for you are sincere.		
He might love you now.		
Due to his high position, he cannot do what he likes.		
He is a virtuous prince that you can trust.		
Hamlet is powerful enough to choose his own wife.		
He cannot choose freely as ordinary people can do, as he has got a position to think of and a country to run.		
If he says he loves you, believe him.		
Consider your honour that is at stake if you now lose your virginity to him.		
Hold back in your affections.		

b) Sum up Laertes' advice to his sister in 1-2 sentences.

c) Describe Ophelia's reaction to Laertes' advice.

SCENE V

9

Horatio has informed Hamlet about the strange apparition. When one night the two friends join Marcellus on his midnight watch, the ghost appears again. Alone with Hamlet, the ghost discloses the whole story.

a) Read the extract (ll. 23-140) and answer the following questions.

1. Why is the ghost doomed to walk the earth by night? ____________________

____

2. What information does he give about his life in purgatory? ____________________

____

3. What was the official version of the former king's death? ____________________

____

4. What does the ghost think about the queen? ____________________

____

5. What was the real reason for the king's death? ____________________

____

6. What troubles the ghost particularly about the end of his life? ____________________

____

7. What does the ghost tell Hamlet to do about his mother? ____________________

____

8. What does the ghost ask Hamlet to do? ____________________

____

9. How does Hamlet react to the ghost's wish? ____________________

____

b) CHOOSE **Group work (3)** You need a narrator, King Hamlet and Claudius. While the narrator reads lines 84 ("Sleeping within my orchard") to 105, the others act out what is described.

OR

Group work (3-6) Imagine you are a film crew shooting this three-minute scene.
Talk about
- what lines you want to use or leave out.
- what shots you use.
- what background music supports the atmosphere of the scene.
- what camera movement you want to employ.
- what special effects to use.

While reading: Act II

SCENE II

1

The King and Queen have sent for Rosencrantz and Guildenstern, two friends of Hamlet's.

a) **Group work (4)** Read the extract (Act II, Scene II, ll. 1-52). Outline the main purpose of the two friends' visit.

b) Discuss the following questions in your group by referring to the text.
   1. Does Claudius come across as a worried stepfather and uncle?
   2. How does Gertrude come across?
   3. Has Claudius sent for Hamlet's friends to put him under surveillance?
   4. Do the two friends come across as individual beings or rather like a double act?
   5. Do Rosencrantz and Guildenstern seem like true and honest friends?

c) Act out the lines bearing in mind what you have discussed.

d) Rosencrantz and Guildenstern always appear together on stage. Talk about why Shakespeare makes them do so.

2

Ophelia has given her father a letter that Hamlet seems to have addressed to her. Now Polonius reads out the letter to the King and Queen.

a) Read Hamlet's letter (ll. 146-165) and summarize it in one sentence.

b) Read the extract ll. 142-228. In class, discuss whether you think this letter is real or simply fabricated by Polonius. If so, what could be the purpose?

c) Polonius tells the King and the Queen what advice he has given his daughter. Read his advice (ll. 188-192) and paraphrase it in your own words.

d) Polonius continues by describing the classical symptoms of lovesickness. Read lines 193-198 and attribute the modern names of the symptoms to the words from the text.

1	sadness	❑ insomnia
2	fast	❑ delirium
3	watch	❑ loss of appetite
4	weakness	❑ depression
5	lightness	❑ weakness

Info

The Elizabethans believed that lovesickness was a serious disease that could lead to madness or even death.

e) Outline Polonius' plan.

f) Analyse Polonius' character: Choose the adjectives that best describe him and find examples from the text to prove your point.

strategic | loyal | loving | worried | cunning | duplicitous | dishonest | contemptuous

3

Hamlet welcomes his two old friends at Elsinore.

a) Read the extract (ll. 322-420), tick the topics they talk about and give evidence.

Topic	✓	Evidence
well-being		
being lucky		
sexual puns		
the reason for their visit		
their prison sentence		
ambition		
nightmares		
honesty		

b) Choose the adjectives that best describe Hamlet's relationship with Rosencrantz and Guildenstern. Find examples from the text to prove your point.

happy | difficult | strained | close | intimate | harmonious | honest | caring | dishonest | deceitful

c) Having seen his friends off, Hamlet contemplates their meeting: Write his inner monologue in which he reflects upon his friends' attitude towards him.

4

Hamlet informs his friends about his state of mind.

a) Read Hamlet's speech (ll. 422-440) and describe his state of mind.

b) Shakespeare is believed to refer to the Globe Theatre in these lines. Look at the picture and identify the allusions to the Globe Theatre in Hamlet's speech.

c) Analyse the language Hamlet uses to describe mankind. Identify the stylistic devices and explain their intended effect on the audience.

anaphora | metaphor | antithesis | alliteration | repetition | parallelism | exclamation

d) **Group work (4-5)** Which tone do you find most appropriate for delivering Hamlet's speech: sarcastic, melancholic, sincere, bitter or awe-struck? Discuss. In your group read out the extract and try out various ways of delivering Hamlet's lines.

5

A group of actors have arrived at Elsinore. Hamlet asks them to perform a play the next night that includes a speech he has written. When they have gone, Hamlet ponders upon the players' ability to feign feelings.

a) Read Hamlet's soliloquy (ll. 745-813). Then structure it and summarize each part in one sentence. The first one has been done for you.

Lines	Summary
747-754	*Hamlet praises the actor's skill to feign emotions.*

b) Describe Hamlet's plan to trick his uncle.

c) Read the info box and identify dramatic irony in the soliloquy.

d) **Group work (5-7)**

1 Talk about
- how Hamlet comes across. Is he impatient, angry or desperate?
- the function of the soliloquy. Bear in mind what you have learned about soliloquies on page 128.

2 Prepare a presentation of the soliloquy, with each of you delivering a part of it.

Info

Dramatic irony

This literary device is used when the audience knows more than the characters in the scene.

While reading: Act III

SCENE I

1

After Rosencrantz and Guildenstern have reported back to the King and Queen, Claudius lets the Queen in on his plan to spy on Hamlet. Then Hamlet enters the stage.

a) Read Hamlet's most famous soliloquy. Then answer the questions below.
   1. What are the two options Hamlet is torn between?
   2. What is the advantage of eternal sleep according to Hamlet?
   3. What uncertainty does Hamlet see in death's sleep?
   4. What injustices does Hamlet list?
   5. What explanation does Hamlet give for why people do not end their lives despite the hardships they endure?
   6. What consequences does the fear of death have for man according to Hamlet?

b) Tick the synopsis that best summarizes Hamlet's soliloquy.
   - ☐ Hamlet contemplates death and all its consequences.
   - ☐ Hamlet meditates on the problems of living and dying.
   - ☐ Hamlet is afraid of all the things that might happen after death.

c) Watch the video and describe how Hamlet comes across in this version. Is this your understanding of the soliloquy? Discuss in class. **Webcode** **DSW-73654-12**

d) **Pair work** CHOOSE Explore the soliloquy with a partner.
   Stand back-to-back, arms linked. One of you, who can see the script, reads out a line, the other one repeats it.
   OR
   You share the speech, alternately speaking small units as a kind of conversation.
   OR
   Think of a simple every-day task, such as painting a wall, cleaning shoes or chopping wood. While you speak small units of the soliloquy alternately, carry out the task.

e) In class, discuss how the activities in d) contribute to a better understanding of the soliloquy.

f) Imagine you are a director and want to turn the soliloquy into a film. Take notes on
   - cinematic devices (field size, camera angle etc.)
   - the scenery and props
   - the background music
   - the way the actor speaks the lines.

2

The King and Polonius eavesdrop on a conversation between Ophelia and Hamlet (ll. 125-224).

a) Outline the conversation between Ophelia and Hamlet.

b) Hamlet treats Ophelia rather harshly. Explain possible reasons for his behaviour.

c) In this extract the themes sin, virtue, appearance and reality play an important role. Find lines in the extract that refer to these themes. Draw a mind map and show how the themes correlate.

d) **Group work (3)**
   1 Discuss what Hamlet really thinks about Ophelia. Does he know he is being spied on? Does he trust Ophelia?
   2 Act out the dialogue: After Hamlet's lines a third student voices his thoughts.

SCENE II

3

Two players, playing the roles of a King and Queen, act out the play in front of the Danish royal court.

a) Read the extract (Scene II, ll. 206-380). Paraphrase the core ideas of the player King and Queen's conversation. Use the characters' perspective as shown in the example.

The player King	*The player Queen*
• *We have been married for 30 years.* • …	• *I hope we will be for another 30 years. I am worried about your health. It is typical of a woman to worry when she loves. I love you deeply and fear for you and your well-being.* • …

b) **Dramatic reading** Read out your results from task a) as a dialogue. Then talk about what gets lost and what becomes clearer.

c) Describe the audience's reactions to the play.

d) Explain the function of the play-within-a-play.

Info

The play-within-a-play

The play-within-a-play is a dramatic convention very popular in Shakespeare's time: a character in a story becomes the narrator of a second story.
As the first professional theatre had only been established some years before in 1567, Elizabethan authors liked to explore the new technical possibilities of the theatre and the nature of entertainment. Besides, the question of the kind of truth that can be told through plays was a focus of the playwrights' interest. As it was widely believed at the time that the theatre had a real impact on its audience, the performance of a crime was believed to force the criminal spectator to admit his or her guilt.
Thus, it is not surprising that a play such as *Hamlet* that evolves around the themes of performance, deception, authenticity, and reality makes use of this literary device. As it also keeps the audience at a distance from the actual crime, it also questions the reliability and the motives of the storyteller.
In general, the inset story or play may have various functions. It may simply offer entertainment, provide an example of what is told in the outer story, have symbolic or psychological significance to the characters of the outer story, or reveal the truth about something that has happened in the outer story. Finally, it may also deflect the audience's attention from a plot twist.

SCENE III

4

After Claudius interrupts and leaves the performance, he considers his next move: He plans to send Hamlet to England with Rosencrantz and Guildenstern accompanying him. Polonius meanwhile plans another ruse: He wants to eavesdrop on a conversation between Gertrude and Hamlet behind a wall hanging.

a) Look up the story of Cain and Abel in the Bible (Genesis 4:11-12) and outline its contents.

b) Read Claudius's soliloquy (Scene 3, ll. 50-86). Then tick the summary that best captures its content.

- ❑ Claudius is torn between the repentance for his crime and his ambition to stay in power. He tries to pray and ask God for forgiveness.
- ❑ Despite his guilty conscience, Claudius does not show any remorse and plots to get rid of his enemies.
- ❑ Claudius is sure that his secret is now revealed and is therefore very unhappy about the murder he has committed. Although he admits his guilt, he cannot show repentance as he is still in possession of Gertrude and the throne.

c) Write an analysis of the language Claudius uses to reveal his state of mind. Follow steps 1-3 and use the language support below.

1 Identify three or four stylistic devices from the box below and explain their functions within the soliloquy.

> **Tip** Start with an introductory sentence which introduces the topic.

alliteration | rhetorical question | accumulation | anaphora | exclamation | simile | antithesis | apostrophe

2 Look at the language Shakespeare uses: is it emotive, offensive, strong or crude? Analyse the choice of words.

3 Explain the function of the reference to Cain and Abel.

Language support

Shakespeare uses/employs ...
He repeatedly employs ...
This can be seen in line xy when he ...
This becomes most evident when he lists ...
Quite a number of words/adjectives refer to ...
The most striking example can be found in ll. ...
It is striking that ...
This stylistic device shows/is a typical example of/illustrates/personifies ...

d) **Group work (4-8): Echoing** Re-read Claudius' soliloquy and underline key words. While one student now reads Claudius' soliloquy the others echo the keywords. Talk about the effect this technique has on the audience. How does it contribute to the atmosphere?

e) Now read Hamlet's reaction when he sees Claudius kneeling (ll. 88-118). Sum up his thoughts in 2-3 sentences.

f) **Pair work: Good angel – bad angel** Work out what Hamlet might tell himself while contemplating his options: should he kill Claudius or not? What arguments does he weigh up? First collect arguments for and against his decision to kill Claudius. Then sit with your backs to each other and perform this conversation of Hamlet's conscience. Use the arguments you have collected as a starting point.

SCENE IV

5

While Polonius is hiding behind a wall hanging, Hamlet chides his mother.

a) Read the extract (Scene IV, ll. 1-48) and answer the following questions:
   1. What is Gertrude supposed to tell Hamlet?
   2. What does Hamlet accuse his mother of?
   3. What does Hamlet want his mother to do?
   4. What does Gertrude think Hamlet wants to do to her?

b) **Pair work: Dramatic reading** Read out lines 15-48. Before you do so, talk about how to read the lines. Is Hamlet agitated, rude or impatient? Is Gertrude angry or afraid? How do the lines each character speaks contribute to the atmosphere?

c) Do you think that Hamlet knows that he has killed someone? Share your ideas in class.

d) Read the continuation of the scene (ll. 49-155). Sum up the arguments Hamlet presents to his mother.

e) **Pair work** Gertrude only has a few lines. Write some more lines for her to show what she really thinks about Hamlet's arguments. Then present the dialogue between mother and son in front of the class. You can have a third student present the additional lines.

While reading: Act IV

SCENE III

1

After the killing of Polonius, Hamlet disappears for a while. Rosencrantz and Guildenstern find him and bring him to the King. Read Act IV, Scene III, ll. 28-104.

a) Hamlet speaks in riddles. But Claudius knows that Hamlet means serious business with what he says. In the grid, note down what Hamlet really means. Then compare your results with a partner's.

Lines	Original text	What Hamlet really means
31	At supper.	
35	Not where he eats, but where he is eaten.	
35-36	A certain convocation of politic worms are e'en at him.	
36-37	Your worm is your only emperor for diet.	
37-38	We fat all creatures else to fat us, and we fat ourselves for maggots.	
38-39	Your fat king and your lean beggar is but variable service, two dishes, but to one table.	
39	That's the end.	
42-43	A man may fish with the worm that hath eat of a king, and eat of the fish that hath fed of that worm.	
47-48	Nothing but to show you how a king may go a progress through the guts of a beggar.	
52	In heaven.	
52	Send thither to see.	
52-53	If your messenger find him not there, seek him I' the other place yourself.	
53-55	But if indeed you find him not within this month, you shall nose him as you go up the stairs into the lobby.	

b) **Group work (4)** Act out the dialogue. One pair of students acts out the original lines. Then the other pair acts out the dialogue with Hamlet speaking the truth. Talk about the changes in atmosphere.
c) Examine to what extent Hamlet carries traits of a jester in this scene.

Info

Jesters

A jester was a popular type of character in Elizabethan drama. Jesters were also known as clowns or fools. They were employed for entertainment in royal and noble households. They usually enjoyed a high reputation and were regarded as witty and wise. In Shakespeare's plays they often function as prophets and wise men who, behind their folly, speak the truth. But there were also natural fools, who were exposed to pratfalls, misfortunes and humiliations in the plays, and whose mere function was to amuse the audience.

d) Talk about why Shakespeare makes Hamlet speak in riddles in this scene.
e) Explain the King's plans for Hamlet.

SCENE V

2

Laertes has stirred up a riot and wants to see the king (Scene V, ll. 157-229).
a) Outline the argument between Laertes and Claudius.
b) Describe Claudius' strategy.
c) Analyse Laertes' behaviour: choose the adjectives that best describe it, find evidence from the text and interpret it. Use a grid like the one below.

aggressive | violent | rash | hasty | thoughtless | hot-headed | incautious | heedless | prudent | audacious | headstrong | revengeful

Adjective	*Evidence (quote and line reference)*	*Interpretation*
...	...	...

d) Use your results from task c) to write an analysis.

3

Laertes meets his sister, who has gone mad.
a) Read the extract (ll. 232-290) and describe Laertes' reaction when he sees his sister.
b) All the flowers and herbs Ophelia mentions carry symbolic associations. Explain why Shakespeare has chosen these flowers.

fennel | pansy | violet | daisy | rue | columbine | rosemary

c) Imagine you are a psychiatrist and Ophelia is brought to you as a new patient. Analyse her state of mind, using the information from the extract, and write your medical report on her.

You may start like this:

____________________________, M.D.
Your name

St Bartholomew's Hospital
West Smithfield
London
EC1A 7BE

Medical report for Ophelia

Diagnosis: Ophelia shows symptoms of ____________________________

Examination results:
Ophelia appears to be ____________________________

4

Ophelia leaves a distressed brother behind.

a) Read the conversation between Laertes and the King (ll. 292-317). Explain how Claudius wants to convince Laertes of his innocence.

b) Write a soliloquy for Claudius' part after Laertes leaves. Consider

- his present situation
- his next steps
- how he means to get rid of Hamlet.

c) Act out your soliloquy in front of the class.

SCENE VII

5

Claudius learns that Hamlet, whom he had sent to England, has returned to Denmark and wants to see him. He asks Laertes for advice.

a) Read the extract (Scene VII, ll. 71-218). Then decide whether the statements are true or false. Give evidence from the text.

	Statement	Evidence	true	false
1	Laertes is looking forward to meeting Hamlet.			
2	Laertes wants Claudius to make peace with Hamlet.			
3	Claudius plots against Hamlet.			
4	According to Claudius Hamlet admires Laertes for his fencing talents.			
5	Claudius wants to arrange a fencing match.			
6	Claudius lets Laertes in on his plan.			
7	Laertes does not want to poison Hamlet.			
8	Claudius suggests a backup plan to be on the safe side.			
9	He wants to manipulate the swords.			

b) Outline the two men's plot.

c) Explain how Claudius characterizes Hamlet and what part this plays in the plan.

d) Analyse Claudius' language to show how he tempts Laertes into avenging his father's death.

6

The Queen has some bad news for the King and Laertes.

a) Read the Queen's description of Ophelia's death (ll. 219-294). Imagine you are a police officer summoned to the scene. Fill in the police report on page 141 based on Gertrude's account.

Police report

Case No. ______________________ Date: ______________

Reporting officer: ______________________________

Incident: ______________________________________

____

____

Detail of event:

1. Who was involved? ____________________________

____

2. What happened? ______________________________

____

3. Where did the incident occur? _________________

____

4. When did the incident happen? ________________

____

5. Why do you think the accused/victim did this? ____

____

Actions taken:

____

____

Summary:

____

____

b) Research the symbolic meanings of the flowers and herbs mentioned in Gertrude's account.
c) Describe the painting *Ophelia* by Sir John Everett Millais (1851-1852) on page 140.
d) Analyse the pictorial elements and their functions. Use the information on the symbolic meaning of the flowers collected in task b).
e) Discuss to what extent the painting reflects the image of nature conveyed in Gertrude's lines.

While reading: Act V

SCENE II

1

Hamlet tells Horatio what happened on his journey to England.

a) Retell Hamlet's story (Act V, Scene II, ll. 1-105) in your own words.
b) Write the letter Hamlet has manipulated.
c) Compare Hamlet's feelings about Rosencrantz and Guildenstern, Claudius, and Laertes.

Language support

When comparing Hamlet's feelings about ... it is striking that ...
Unlike his feelings towards ... Hamlet seems to be ...
By comparison with/in contrast to/compared to x, y seems ...

Hamlet's feelings		
Rosencrantz and Guildenstern	**Claudius**	**Laertes**

d) **Extra** Do some research on Tom Stoppard's play *Rosencrantz and Guildenstern Are Dead* (1966). Find out about
- the main characters
- the storyline
- the themes.

2

Shortly before the fencing match with Laertes begins, Hamlet considers his options.

a) Read the extract (ll. 262-287). Tick the description that best captures Hamlet's attitude towards providence and give evidence from the text.
- ❑ Hamlet believes he can tempt providence and fend off his own fate.
- ❑ Hamlet believes in divine providence: whatever is destined to happen will happen. Man can only be prepared by meeting death with the right frame of mind.
- ❑ Hamlet has grave misgivings about the fencing match. But he does not want to appear superstitious like a woman.

b) The Queen has asked Hamlet and Laertes to chat politely before the match. Outline their chat (ll. 294-323) in 2-3 sentences.
c) Discuss Hamlet's explanation for why he has killed Polonius.
d) **Pair work** The audience knows that Laertes plans to kill Hamlet. One of you reads Laertes' lines (ll. 315-323) and pauses at each punctuation mark, the other one fills the pauses by outlining what Laertes might really be thinking. Use the grid on page 143.

Original text	What might Laertes really be thinking?
I am satisfied in nature,	
Whose motive, in this case, should stir me most	
To my revenge. But in my terms of honour	
I stand aloof, and will no reconcilement,	
Till by some elder masters, of known honour,	
I have a voice and precedent of peace,	
To keep my name ungored. But till that time,	
I do receive your offered love like love,	
And will not wrong it.	

3

The fencing match begins.

a) Read the extract (ll. 371-518) and put the events into the correct order by adding numbers to the grid.

Number	Event
	Hamlet wounds Laertes.
	The Queen dies.
	The Queen takes Hamlet's cup of wine and drinks from it.
	Hamlet wounds the King.
	The King raises a cup of wine and offers another to Hamlet.
	Laertes forgives Hamlet and dies.
	Hamlet prevents Horatio from committing suicide and asks him to tell his story.
	Hamlet and Laertes accidentally exchange their rapiers.
	Laertes reveals the treacherous plot.
	Hamlet and Laertes start fighting.
	The King dies.
	Hamlet rejects the cup.
	Laertes wounds Hamlet.
	Hamlet makes the King drink from the poisoned cup.

b) **Pair work**

1 Discuss why Gertrude drinks from Hamlet's poisoned cup of wine. Does she know it is poisoned? Or is it a mere accident? One partner argues that Gertrude commits suicide. The other argues that she does not know the cup is poisoned.

2 Talk about how the different interpretations change our attitude towards Gertrude.

c) **Group work (5-6)** In this final scene, the whole tragedy unfolds. Try several ways of acting out the scene:

- Have one student tell the story while the others act it out.
- Perform a mime.
- Perform a "fast-forward" version.
- Perform the scene backwards.

Talk about the different effects the ways of acting out the scene create.

4

When Hamlet is dying, he votes for Fortinbras as the next King of Denmark.

a) Read the extract. Then summarize the major events (ll. 526-598).

b) Hamlet's last words, "the rest is silence", have been widely discussed. Do Hamlet's last words imply a personal as well as a political message? Explain your interpretation.

c) Horatio lists the incidents that he will tell Fortinbras about. Explain what events he refers to.

Lines	Incident	Explanation
569	carnal [...] acts	
569	bloody [...] acts	
569	unnatural acts	
570	accidental judgements	
570	casual slaughters	
571	deaths put on by cunning [...] cause	
571	deaths put on by [...] forced cause	

d) Tell Horatio's story.

e) According to Aristotle, a famous Greek philosopher and critic (384-322 BC), the ideal tragic ending is the necessary consequence of all the action that preceded it, in other words the final outcome somehow reflects the story as a whole. Discuss to what extent this is true for this play.

Post-reading

1 CHOOSE **Group work**

Decide which are the most important scenes or events of the play. Use a symbol or picture to indicate what each scene is about, write a headline for the scene and summarize it in one sentence. The first event has been done for you. Then present your ideas to the class.

A ghost appears				
A ghost appears to Horatio, who then decides to inform Prince Hamlet about the apparition.				

OR

Decide which scenes or events in the play are the most important ones. Talk about how you can present them. Then act out each scene in 1 minute. One student is the timekeeper. Explain why you have chosen these scenes.

2 **Group work (8)**

a) Prepare a poster for each character: Hamlet, Claudius, Gertrude, Polonius, Laertes, Ophelia, Horatio and Fortinbras.
  - First find quotations typical of the character.
  - Then analyse his or her character.
  - Finally describe his or her role in the play.

b) Present your posters in a Gallery Walk.

3

Read the info box on obituaries and write an obituary for one of the characters that dies during the play. Use the information you have collected in task 2.

Info

Obituary

An obituary is a news article that announces a well-known person's recent death and informs the reader about this person's life and achievements. It has become a quite popular subgenre in British and American newspapers. It consists of a headline, a sub-heading, the name of the author, a main part and a concluding paragraph. An obituary does not always praise the person but may also show the mysterious and indecent sides of the person.

4

Hamlet raises many universal questions and deals with many universal themes that have interested people across centuries and cultures.

a) **Pair work** List as many of these questions and themes you can think of and compare your ideas with a partner's. Together, settle on one question or theme and explore it in more depth. Give evidence from the text.

b) Write an essay about your question or theme and present it to the class.

5

Choose the quote you like best. Briefly outline the context of the quote and explain your choice.

1. Frailty, thy name is Woman (Act I, Scene II, line 172)
2. Neither a borrower nor a lender be. For loan oft loses both itself and friend and borrowing dulls the edge of husbandry. (Act I, Scene III, lines 89-91)
3. Something is rotten in the state of Denmark. (Act I, Scene IV, line 134)
4. Though this be madness, yet there is method in't. (Act II, Scene II, line 291)
5. What a piece of work is a man. How noble in reason, how infinite in faculty, in form and moving how express and admirable, in action how like an angel, in apprehension how like a god – the beauty of the world, the paragon of animals. (Act II, Scene II, lines 433-437)
6. they [i.e. the players] are the abstract and brief chronicles of the time. (Act II, Scene II, lines 708-709)
7. To be, or not to be, that is the question. Whether 'tis nobler in the mind to suffer the slings and arrows of outrageous fortune, or to take arms against a sea of troubles, and by opposing end them? (Act III, Scene I, lines 90-94)
8. Our wills and fates do so contrary run that our devices still are overthrown. Our thoughts are ours, their ends none of our own. (Act III, Scene II, lines 293-295)
9. The lady doth protest too much, methinks. (Act III, Scene II, line 321)
10. This is I, Hamlet the Dane. (Act V, Scene I, lines 346-347)

6

Imagine you are a director and asked to turn Shakespeare's *Hamlet* into a modern film version. Outline this version.

1. Title: ______________________________

2. Genre (e.g. western, thriller, horror film): ______________________________

3. Setting (Where and when does the story take place?): ______________________________

____

4. Cast: actors for the main roles

______________________________ as Hamlet

______________________________ as ______________________________

______________________________ as ______________________________

______________________________ as ______________________________

______________________________ as ______________________________

______________________________ as ______________________________

______________________________ as ______________________________

7

Pair work You want to pitch your film version to a production company.

a) Prepare the pitch, in which you
- summarize the original plot of the play
- present your reasons for making this kind of film
- talk about the relevance of the story for modern audiences
- outline the main ideas of your film version.

b) Present your pitch to the class. The other students function as board members of the production company. After everyone has presented a pitch, vote for the best one.

Info

Pitch

A pitch is a short oral presentation of an idea for a film or TV series, given by a director or screenwriter to convince a film producer to fund the project. As time is money, the presentation must be short and to the point.

Fate vs. free will

FREEDOM AND RESPONSIBILITY

1

Is life determined by fate or free will? In other words, have you ever wondered if you have control over your actions, and if so, to what extent? Or are your actions determined by some other forces? Philosophers have been arguing about these issues for thousands of years.

a) **Pair work** Is the boy in the photo jumping into the water based on his own free will? Or was his decision determined by any exterior force? With a partner, exchange your views on this issue.

b) Read this extract from an entry in the online *Encyclopaedia Britannica* to explore the opposing views of *free will* and *determinism*. Then match the sentences on the next page to test your knowledge.

Problem of moral responsibility

by Peter Singer and Maya Eddon

Problem of moral responsibility, the problem of reconciling the belief that people are morally responsible for what they do with the apparent fact that humans do not have free will because their actions are causally determined. It is an ancient and enduring philosophical puzzle.

Freedom and responsibility

Historically, most proposed solutions to the problem of moral responsibility have attempted to establish that humans do have free will. But what does free will consist of? When people make decisions or perform actions, they usually feel as though they are choosing or acting freely. A person may decide, for example, to buy apples instead of oranges, to vacation in France rather than in Italy, or to call a sister in Nebraska instead of a brother in Florida. On the other hand, there are at least some situations in which people seem not to act freely, as when they are physically coerced or mentally or emotionally manipulated. One way to formalize the intuitive idea of free action is to say that a person acts freely if it is true that he could have acted otherwise. Buying apples is ordinarily a free action because in ordinary circumstances one can buy oranges instead; nothing forces one to buy apples or prevents one from buying oranges.

Yet the decisions a person makes are the result of his desires, and his desires are determined by his circumstances, his past experiences, and his psychological and personality traits – his dispositions, tastes, temperament, intelligence, and so on. Circumstances, experiences, and traits in this sense are obviously the result of many factors outside the individual's control, including his upbringing and perhaps even his genetic makeup. If this is correct, then a person's actions may ultimately be no more the result of free will than his eye colour.

The existence of free will seems to be presupposed by the notion of moral responsibility. Most people would agree that a person cannot be morally responsible for actions that he could not help but perform. Moreover, moral praise and blame, or reward and punishment, seem to make sense only on the assumption that the agent in question is morally responsible. These considerations seem to imply a choice between two implausible alternatives: either (1) people have free will, in which case a person's actions are not determined by his circumstances, past experiences, and psychological and personality traits, or (2) people do not have free will, in which case no one is ever morally responsible for what he does. This dilemma is the problem of moral responsibility.

Determinism

Determinism is the view that, given the state of the universe (the complete physical properties of all its parts) at a certain time and the laws of nature operative in the universe at that time, the state of the universe at any subsequent time is completely determined. No subsequent state of the universe can be other than what it is. Since human actions, at an appropriate level of description, are part of the universe, it follows that humans cannot act otherwise than they do; free will is impossible. [...]

Philosophers and scientists who believe that the universe is deterministic and that determinism is incompatible with free will are called "hard" determinists. Since moral responsibility seems to require free will, hard determinism implies that no one is morally responsible for his actions. Although the conclusion is strongly counterintuitive, some hard determinists have insisted that the weight of philosophical argument requires that it be accepted. There is no alternative but to reform the intuitive beliefs in freedom and moral responsibility. Other hard determinists, acknowledging that such reform is scarcely feasible, hold that there may be social benefits to feeling and exhibiting moral emotions, even though the emotions themselves are based on a fiction. Such benefits are reason enough for holding fast to prephilosophical beliefs about free will and moral responsibility, according to these thinkers.

1 When people make decisions ☐
2 For the believer in free will, the individuals ☐
3 When you believe in free will ☐
4 Science is based on ☐
5 Determinists believe that ☐
6 According to determinism a decision made by somebody is ☐
7 Actions, in this view, are triggered by ☐
8 When people do not have free will, ☐

A the necessary result of predetermined developments and conditions.
B deterministic principles.
C they usually think they act and choose freely.
D everything that happens, happens for a reason and could not happen differently.
E a person's desires, beliefs and temperament.
F you think you are able to make choices in which the outcome has not been determined by past events.
G they cannot be held responsible for their actions.
H make conscious choices.

c) Check your knowledge by describing the cartoon and explaining its message.

Annotations
merely = only
naught = nothing

WHAT THE ELIZABETHANS BELIEVED IN

2

Analyse this picture, showing the *Wheel of Fortune*, which was a very widely held idea in Shakespeare's day. You can use these words and phrases.

fate | at random | a change in fortune | to be subject to

3

Another popular conception at the time was the *Great Chain of Being*. Read the statements on the next page. Then use them to explain the picture below them.

1. A popular belief was that everything in the world had a set position in a great hierarchy. They called this belief the Great Chain of Being. If this order and positioning was upset in any way, people believed that the harmony of their whole society would be at stake.

2. Many Elizabethans believed that certain dualities existed in the Great Chain of Being. One belief they had was that the king was as important to the state as the sun was to the sky. This meant that if something seemed to be wrong in the heavens, this would worry rulers, as it could be reflected on earth.

3. Marriage could be used to help make a family wealthy or increase their social standing. Women were usually not consulted about their marriages and their feelings were not taken into account.

4. It was believed that if the structure was broken in any way – for example, if someone killed the king, if the king abdicated, or if someone married outside of their social class – then chaos would ensue and everything would fall apart.

5. It was the king's supreme responsibility to enforce and uphold this social order because he was believed to be the chosen representative of God on earth. To do something against the king, such as committing treason, was regarded as the equivalent of committing a mortal sin against God, and could lead to intense problems and chaos on earth.

4

Bearing in mind the *Wheel of Fortune* and the *Great Chain of Being*, explain how the Elizabethans regarded the issues of fate and free will.

Fate vs. free will in *Hamlet*

1

a) Read Act I, Scene V, ll. 23-116 again. Outline King Hamlet's murder in 2-3 sentences.
b) Discuss the significance of King Hamlet's murder for the state of Denmark according to the Elizabethan world view.
c) Talk about possible reasons why Shakespeare did not set his play in England.

2

a) Read the following extracts from the play and pick out aspects from these lines that underline the Elizabethan world view as described on pages 149-150. Use the right-hand column for your notes.

Extracts	Notes
His greatness weighed, his will is not his own, For he himself is subject to his birth. He may not, as unvalued persons do, Carve for himself, for on his choice depends The safety and health of this whole state, And therefore must his choice be circumscribed Unto the voice and yielding of that body Whereof he is the head. (Act I, Scene III, lines 26-33)	
Sir, in my heart there was a kind of fighting That would not let me sleep. Methought I lay Worse than the mutines in the bilboes. Rashly – And praised be rashness for it – let us know Our indiscretion sometimes serves us well When our deep plots do pall, and that should teach us There's a divinity that shapes our ends, Rough-hew them how we will – (Act V, Scene II, lines 8-15)	
I shall win at the odds. But thou wouldst not think how ill all's here about my heart. But it is no matter. [...] It is but foolery, but it is such a kind of gaingiving, as would perhaps trouble a woman. [...] We defy augury. There's a special providence in the fall of a sparrow. If it be now, 'tis not to come. If it be not to come, it will be now. If it be not now, yet it will come. The readiness is all. Since no man has aught of what he leaves, what is't to leave betimes? Let be. (Act V, Scene II, lines 272/273, 277/278, 283-287)	

b) Explain the different attitudes towards fate and free will expressed in these extracts.

c) Is the destiny of these characters shaped by fate or by other factors, such as their personalities, chance or other people's ruses? Discuss this question in class. Take some notes beforehand in order to be able to give evidence from the play.

Polonius	Ophelia

Laertes	Claudius

Gertrude	Hamlet

Rosencrantz and Guildenstern	Fortinbras

3

Based on your findings from the previous tasks, write an essay. Here are some ideas:

- Fate vs. free will in Shakespeare's time
- Why Hamlet had to die at the end of the play
- Why Rosencrantz and Guildenstern die

4 CHOOSE

Pair work On page 148, task 1 you have learned about the philosophical concepts of free will and determinism. Imagine a modern conversation between a libertarian (representative of the concept of free will) and a determinist arguing about the question whether Hamlet was free in his decisions and actions. Carry out this discussion.

OR

Group work Discuss how our view of the world has changed in comparison to the Elizabethan world view.

The role(s) of women

ROYAL WIVES TODAY

1

What role does the British royal family play in modern society? Haven't the royals become something of the past? And what part do the women play in all this?

a) Identify the women in the photos and find out what role they play or used to play in British society.

b) Discuss to what extent they can be seen as role models. → **S6:** How to write a discussion/comment

THE ROLE(S) OF WOMEN IN SHAKESPEARE'S TIME

2 Pair work

What role did women play in Shakespeare's time? Don't forget that a woman, Elizabeth I, ruled England.

a) Read the articles about women in Shakespeare's time below. One of you reads text A, the other one text B. Sum up the main arguments of your text and then present them to your partner.

b) Compare the role of women in Shakespeare's time to that of women in Britain today. You can use some of these words and phrases

as to | whereas | while | similarly | in contrast to | unlike | compared to | in comparison with

A Audience and social attitudes: Women

In Elizabethan times women belonged to their fathers (or their brothers if their father died), and then to their husbands. Women could not own property of their own. This is one of the reasons Queen Elizabeth never married – she did not want to give up her power to a man.

The only exceptions were widows – women whose husbands had died. A widow was in charge of her own life and property, but would be likely to marry again to find someone to protect her and to be the legal guardian to her children.

Women were allowed to marry from the age of 12 in Shakespeare's time, but often only women from wealthy families would marry so young. In the play *Romeo and Juliet*, Juliet is 13, but her mother says by that age she was already married with a child. Many marriages were arranged for the good of the family and small children might be "betrothed"[1] to each other in order to join the families together before they were old enough to get married. Many women did not marry until their mid-20s. Men had to be able to support a household when they married. [...]

Annotations

[1] **betrothed** = promised

B Shakespeare's presentation of women

by Lee Jamieson, 4 August 2017

Shakespeare's presentation of women in his plays demonstrates his feelings about women and their roles in society. [...]

It's well known that women weren't allowed on the stage during Shakespeare's active years. All of his famous female roles like Desdemona and Juliet were in fact once played by men!

Women in Shakespeare's plays are often underestimated. While they were clearly restricted by their social roles, the Bard showed how women could influence the men around them. His plays showed the difference in expectations between upper and lower class women of the time. High-born women are presented as "possessions" to be passed between fathers and husbands. In most cases, they are socially restricted and unable to explore the world around them without chaperones[1]. Many of these women were coerced[2] and controlled by the men in their lives. Lower-born women were allowed more freedom in their actions precisely because they are seen as less important than higher-born women.

Annotations

[1] **chaperone** = older woman who accompanies a younger unmarried woman to keep an eye on her

[2] to **coerce** = to force

The role(s) of women in *Hamlet*

1

Some critics claim that Gertrude's character raises more questions than it answers.

a) **Group work (4)** Study the extracts labelled *The role(s) of women* on pages 20/21, 22, 40/41, 58-60, 81, 93-97, 110-116, 121, 150 and 182/183 of your *Hamlet* edition. Choose one of the questions below and discuss it in your group. Try to find evidence from the play to prove your ideas. Then present your results in class.

1. Did Gertrude have an affair with Claudius before her first husband's death?
2. Did she love her first husband?
3. Does she know about the plots Claudius is involved in?
4. Did she marry Claudius for love, or did she just want to keep her social position?
5. Does she believe her son, or does she think he is mad?
6. Does she think critically about her own actions and situation?

b) **Pair work** One of you takes Gertrude's role shortly after she got married to Claudius. The other one is the psychiatrist who wants to find out about her feelings, desires and fears. Use the questions below to prepare a scene showing this meeting between Gertrude and her psychiatrist.

- What is Gertrude's present situation like?
- What does Gertrude know about Claudius?
- How does she feel about him?
- Does she love or loathe him?
- What does this feeling mean to her?
- How does she envision her future life with Claudius?
- What kind of relationship does she have to her son?
- What are her greatest hopes and fears?

c) Act out the scene in front of the class.

2

Hot seat Study the extracts labelled *The role(s) of women* on pages 20/21, 22, 58-60, 81, 110-116, 121, 150 and 182/183. Then prepare a hot seat: One student steps into the role of Gertrude, another into the role of Hamlet. The other students ask them questions about their relationship.

3

Ophelia is often portrayed as a passive victim, whom men tell what to do.

a) Study the extracts labelled *The role(s) of women* on pages 29/30, 31/32, 51/52, 58-60, 81, 82-84, 93-97, 136-138, 141/142 and 154/155 of your *Hamlet* edition. Then analyse Ophelia's relationships to the three men. Use the grid for your findings.

Language support

obedient | passive | to keep quiet about | submissive | patient | meek | lamblike | deferential | docile | long-suffering | affectionate | grief-stricken | hurt | dutiful

Polonius	
Laertes	
Hamlet	

b) Study the photos carefully. Choose an actress that fits your idea of Ophelia best. Explain your decision.

Helen Mirren (1970)

Joanne Pearce (1992)

Daisy Ridley (2018)

Natalie Simpson (2016)

c) **Pair work** Imagine you were a director and had to re-interpret Ophelia's role for today's audiences. Would she still be passive and obedient or rather emancipated and self-confident? Rewrite a scene with Ophelia, in which her more modern personality comes across. Then act out the scene.

4

Some scholars claim that the women in *Hamlet* are all powerless victims. Considering your findings from the previous tasks, discuss this claim.

Questions of morality

1 CHOOSE **Pair work**

1 Have you ever thought about taking revenge? Where does revenge still take place? Can taking revenge ever be justified? Discuss these questions with a partner.
2 Find out what different legal systems and holy books of different religions say about taking revenge.
3 Present your findings to the class.
4 Is your motto "An eye for an eye" or rather "Turn the other cheek"? Explain.

OR

1 Have you ever thought about deceiving someone? In which areas does deception play a role? Is deception always negative? Discuss these questions with a partner.
2 Find out what different legal systems and holy books of different religions say about deceiving people.
3 Present your findings to the class.
4 Can a white lie be justified? Explain your view.

2

Although the Elizabethans regarded revenge as a crime and a sin and the revenger's soul was believed to be condemned to eternal torment, the genre of revenge tragedy was immensely popular during Shakespeare's lifetime.

a) Read the info box about revenge tragedies and apply the characteristics to *Hamlet*. Give evidence from the play.

Info

Revenge tragedy

The earliest English revenge tragedy, *The Spanish Tragedy*, was written by Thomas Kyd around 1582. Other well-known revenge tragedies are Christopher Marlowe's *The Jew of Malta* (1589–90), William Shakespeare's *Titus Andronicus* (1588) and Thomas Middleton's *The Revenger's Tragedy* (around 1606).
The most common characteristics of a revenge tragedy are:

1. a play-within-a-play
2. madness
3. the supernatural (e.g. a ghost who forces the protagonist to avenge his death)
4. disguises
5. violent murders
6. a once-noble protagonist who degenerates
7. complex plotting
8. hesitant behaviour
9. the display of melancholy
10. a fifth act in which many characters are killed

b) EXTRA Research the revenge tragedies mentioned in the info box. Give a brief outline of the respective plays and compare them to *Hamlet*: Where do they show similarities and where do they differ?

c) Talk about how the different characteristics of a revenge tragedy can be used to explore the questions of morality in *Hamlet*.

3

Use the information from the info box to show to what extent Hamlet or another character from the play can be called a tragic hero. Give evidence from the play.

Info

Tragedy

According to the Greek philosopher Aristotle (384–322 BC), a tragedy is a play that possesses magnitude and imitates events that evoke pity and fear. Its plot is complex, involving reversal (a changing situation) and recognition (a change from ignorance to knowledge).
The tragic hero is not of outstanding moral excellence but is held in great esteem and enjoys great fortune. He is nobler and more refined than ordinary people. The change to bad fortune that he must undergo is the result of an error of some kind (Greek: *hamartia*). This error has been interpreted in different ways. Some modern scholars call it a moral flaw or tragic flaw, others, however, interpret it as an intellectual error made in ignorance or through misjudgement, a misinterpretation of the circumstances.

4

a) Read the extracts of the play that are labelled *Questions of morality* in your *Hamlet* edition. You find them on pages 19, 22, 39-42, 55/56, 62-64, 71/72, 82, 107/108, 110-113, 114-116, 132/133, 139-141, 151/152, 153/154, 173-175, 179/180, 180/181 and 182-185. Then use the grid to collect information on the different characters regarding the various aspects of morality of the play. Use the last column to analyse another character that you consider relevant in this regard.

	Hamlet	Claudius	Gertrude	
moral/ immoral behaviour				
reasons for revenge				
examples of betrayal and deception				
moral principles/ attitude towards morality				

b) Rank the different characters according to a scale ranging from 1 (morally good) to 6 (morally bad) and explain your decisions.
c) Explain the functions of these characters and their moral attitudes for the play.
d) Compare Hamlet, Laertes and Fortinbras in terms of the ways they deal with their desire for revenge.
e) EXTRA **Group work (5)** Host a talk show. Each of you plays a character you have analysed in a) and b) and one of you acts as the talk show host. The host and the other students from your class as the audience can ask the characters questions about their moral principles.

5

Thinking hats discussion Imagine: shortly before the fencing match is arranged, Hamlet contemplates his options. Discuss the following question: should Hamlet take revenge?

a) **Group work (3-5)**: **Think-pair-share** Form 6 groups. Each group considers the problem from a different point of view.

white	yellow	black	red	green	blue
neutral What are the facts and figures?	**optimist** What are positive aspects?	**pessimist** What is wrong with the idea?	**emotional** How do I feel about this?	**creative** What alternatives do I have?	**organizing** What steps must I take?

1 Think: On your own, consider the problem and take some notes.
2 Pair: Exchange your ideas and prepare a short presentation to give to the group.
3 Share: Share your ideas within your group.

b) Stage the thinking hats discussion.

6

Write an essay on one of these topics. Refer to extracts from the play where appropriate.

- How does Shakespeare point out the ethical implications of taking revenge in *Hamlet*?
- When trying to find out the truth about a crime, does this end justify all means?
- Does revenge pay?
- Can betrayal or deception ever be justified?
- Is Hamlet too good to live in this world? Do his noble qualities and his sensitivity lead to his downfall?

TEXTQUELLEN

6 Quote by Martin Luther King Jr.: "Forgiveness is ..." San Francisco: Goodreads, Inc. https://www.goodreads.com/quotes/57037-forgiveness-is-not-an-occasional-act-it-is-a-constant (19.04.2022)

6 Quote by Wil Zeus, *Sun Beyond the Clouds:* "Always forgive, but ..." San Francisco: Goodreads, Inc. https://www.goodreads.com/quotes/247513-always-forgive-but-never-forget-else-you-will-be-a?page=4 (19.04.2022)

6 Quote by Gordon B. Hinckley: "The whole essence ..." https://www.allgreatquotes.com/authors/gordon-b-hinckley/page/3/ (19.04.2022)

6 Quote by Deb Caletti: "I guess forgiveness ..." San Francisco: Goodreads, Inc. https://www.goodreads.com/quotes/75628-i-guess-forgiveness-like-happiness-isn-t-a-final-destination-you (19.04.2022)

21 f. Geoff Dyer: "Who's afraid of influence?" In: *The Guardian*, 22.09.2001. Copyright Guardian News & Media Ltd 2022. https://www.theguardian.com/books/2001/sep/22/fiction.ianmcewan (24.02.2022)

24 f. "What is Britishness?" | "Identification with Britishness." In: *Citizenship and Belonging: What is Britishness? A research study*. London: Commission for Racial Equality, November 2005, S. 6–7. http://www.ethnos.co.uk/pdfs/9_what_is_britishness_CRE.pdf (03.05.2022)

25 f. „Wie ein Schülerlied Großbritannien entzweit – ‚Untersteht euch, meinem Kind das Gehirn zu waschen!'" Jörg Schindler, DER SPIEGEL 24.06.2021. https://www.spiegel.de/ausland/grossbritannien-wie-ein-patriotisches-schuelerlied-das-land-entzweit-a-0175d1c6-39a6-43a3-96a0-8f624da32b9a (24.02.2022)

28 Quote by Ivanka Trump, *The Trump Card*: "Perception is ..." In: *Vanity Fair*, 24.04.2017. https://www.vanityfair.com/hollywood/2017/04/john-oliver-jared-kushner-ivanka-trump-last-week-tonight (02.03.2022)

30–35 Nafissa Thompson-Spires: "Heads of the Colored People: Four Fancy Sketches, Two Chalk Outlines, and No Apology." In: Nafissa Thompson-Spires: *Heads of the Colored People*. London: Vintage/Penguin Random House 2019, S. 1–14.

37 f. Anonymous: "I was very interested in ...", 26.03.2021 | Danielle Hawthorne: "Nafissa Thompson-Spires is ...", 26.03.2021 | Phoenix Johnson: "Thompson-Spires has a special ...", 25.03.2021 – Haley Reading (Group 1) Nafissa Thompson-Spires's "Heads of the Colored People" Comments. Hrsg.: Professor Howard Rambsy II, Edwardsville, Illinois, USA, 24.03.2021. https://www.culturalfront.org/2021/03/haley-reading-group-1-nafissa-thompson_24.html?m=1 (18.04.2022)

39–47 Camille Acker: "Mambo Sauce." In: Camille Acker: *Training School For Negro Girls*. New York: The Feminist Press 2018, S. 129–158.

52 "Ethnic identity." In: *APA (American Psychological Association) Dictionary of Psychology*. Washington, DC: American Psychological Association. https://dictionary.apa.org/ethnic-identity (20.04.2022)

52 Quote by Malcolm X, *The Autobiography of Malcolm X*: "I believe in recognizing ..." San Francisco: Goodreads, Inc. https://www.goodreads.com/work/quotes/47400-the-autobiography-of-malcolm-x (02.03.2022)

63 Quote from the film *The Founder* (2016): "Persistence. ... all day long." MovieQuotesandMore, Hrsg.: Parissa Janaraghi. https://www.moviequotesandmore.com/the-founder-best-quotes/ (09.05.2022)

63 Quotes from the film *The Founder* (2016): "McDonald's can be the new American church. ... One word, persistence." MagicalQuote: https://www.magicalquote.com/moviequotes/mcdonalds-can-be-the-new-american-church/ (09.05.2022)

68 ff. Marinela Potor: „Wie nachhaltig ist McDonald's Deutschland wirklich?" Berlin: BASIC thinking GmbH, 30.03.2021. https://www.basicthinking.de/blog/2021/03/30/mcdonalds-deutschland-klimacheck/ (02.05.2022)

71 "11 Facts LGBT Life In America." New York: Do Something, Inc. https://www.dosomething.org/us/facts/11-facts-lgbt-life-america (11.05.2022) (verändert)

78 f. Amnesty International: "Discrimination." © 2022 Amnesty International. https://www.amnesty.org/en/what-we-do/discrimination/ (12.05.2022)

80 "Diversity Wheel." Adapted from: Loden, Marilyn & Rosener, Judy, "Workforce America! Managing Employee Diversity as a Vital Resource." McGraw-Hill Professional Publishing, 1990. (verändert)

88 "The 12 Steps of AA." Alcoholics Anonymous Great Britain and English Speaking Continental Europe. https://www.alcoholics-anonymous.org.uk/about-aa/the-12-steps-of-aa (13.05.2022)

88 Quote from the film Boy Erased (2018): "Your father's asked me ... Any questions?" MovieQuotesandMore, Hrsg.: Parissa Janaraghi. https://www.moviequotesandmore.com/boy-erased-best-movie-quotes/ (13.05.2022)

89 Quotes from the film *Boy Erased* (2018): Sarah: "I would look at other girls ... forgive me all these things." | Gary: "Dear Heavenly Father ... path to righteousness." In: BOY ERASED (2018) – FULL TRANSCRIPT. https://subslikescript.com/movie/Boy_Erased-7008872 (13.05.2022)

90 Quote from the film *Boy Erased* (2018): "I imagine I'm him sometimes. ..." MovieQuotesandMore, Hrsg.: Parissa Janaraghi. https://www.moviequotesandmore.com/boy-erased-best-movie-quotes/ (13.05.2022)

95 Quote from the film *Boy Erased* (2018): "I wish none of this had ever happened. ..." MovieQuotesandMore, Hrsg.: Parissa Janaraghi. https://www.moviequotesandmore.com/boy-erased-best-movie-quotes/ (16.05.2022)

95 f. „Gesetz gegen „Homoheiler" – Ein Meilenstein für Deutschland." Markus Kowalski im Gespräch mit Stephan Karkowsky. Köln: Deutschlandfunk Kultur, Deutschlandradio, 07.05.2020. https://www.deutschlandfunkkultur.de/gesetz-gegen-homoheiler-ein-meilenstein-fuer-deutschland-100.html (16.05.2022)

97 f. Salomé Kofler: „Was ist ein Ally?" München: Zeitjung.de, Z-LIVE GmbH, 11.08.2020. https://www.zeitjung.de/was-ist-ein-ally-gesellschaft-allyship-engagement-definitionen/ (16.05.2022)